Praise for

Living Waters
A Journey of Faith and Discovery
Connecting the Past with the Present

Judy Davis is a passionate disciple of the Kingdom of God. Her book is a compilation of various aspects of her personal journey of discovery of not only her ancestry, she is a descendant of Pocahontas, but also her understanding of God's prophetic purposes of redemption. Using her experiences as a missionary, an intercessor, and leader of a Dance and Banner Worship team she interweaves layers of her own story with references to Church and Jewish history, theology and God's purposes for the Church and the Jewish people. Judy has done her homework and has supplied the reader with many references that you can use in your own research and study. I believe this book will not only bless you but educate you as well.
    Dr. Howard Morgan
    Kingdom Ministries International
    howardmorganministries.com

Living Waters is a journey of one person's experiences shared in particular while visiting the nation of Israel. Judy's senses come alive to paint a picture of the reality of her time spent in Israel—from Jerusalem to Judea, Samaria to Galilee, and other destinations. She chose the way of a servant by coming and volunteering to do humanitarian aid work with The Joseph Storehouse. By doing so, it's as if the heavens opened up around Jerusalem while a smile looked down upon Judy with happiness and joy. This book is a real testimony of how one person's experience can impact others.
    Barry and Batya Segal
    Vision for Israel | The Joseph Storehouse
    visionforisrael.com

I love this book! It was so special to get to know Judy and learn of her many missions trips. I know our Abba is very happy she said "yes" to His call to missions and went...not so many do. I also loved how generations past affect us and that we carry their authority with us in the present to be able to repent and restore the destiny that our Abba meant for us to walk in. *Living Waters* will encourage you. Thank you, Judy, for all you have done for the Kingdom!

Jean Mabry, Director Bezalel School
Benote Tzion & For Zion's Sake Dance ministries
zionsake.org

Judy Davis has obtained the high mark of excellence in this powerful, captivating and dynamic book. You will be blessed as you journey with her through this wonderful presentation of passionate love of true worship of our Jewish Messiah. Her delightful accounts of her numerous mission trips abroad connected with history and the supernatural will spark a flame to find God's purpose in your own life!

Jim Jackson, President
CBU Ministries International, Montreat, NC
cbu.org

Judy Davis is an extraordinary woman. As she struggled against false and discouraging doctrines being presented in her church, she realized that she could not and would not compromise the truth of God's Word. She made the decision to step out of the denomination she was in and fully embrace the Charismatic Renewal sweeping Christianity. Holy Spirit fire began to flame up in her life as she yielded to the Spirit's direction. From that step of faith she came to understand the importance of her Jewish Roots and the importance of blessing Israel. I have known Judy for many years as a steadfast woman of God and a very gifted worshipper with banners and silks. This book will be an inspiration to all, especially those who are seeking to find their place in God's plan for their life. Please read this book—I know you will be blessed.

Dee Baxter, Bible Teacher
President Baxter Bible Ministries, LaFayette, GA
baxterbibleministries.org

Generations to come will thank Judy for this brilliant work. She opens doors for readers to gain new perspectives while exploring her life experiences. Judy's insights into an important history of faith and dedication are refreshing. I highly recommend this book!
Hannele Pardain
cfi-usa.org

Living Waters shows Judy's love for literature as well as her passion for making a difference in the world. I had the pleasure of hosting Judy at one of my Free to Create art retreats and was able to witness her creativity and love of life first hand. Her poems strike to the heart and soul, just like her very own account of personal discovery. She weaves her poems with historical and spiritual facts in such a beautiful manner. This book is indeed a unique blend of literature and history. It is as colorful as each of Judy's trips to the different parts of the world.
Janice VanCronkhite
Artist, speaker, instructor, author
JvcArtworks.com

Judy's vulnerability in showing the struggles in understanding God's messages to us is refreshing. Her steps of faith led her to many places. In 1998 she joined us in Israel for our Integrity Music recording with Paul Wilbur and a special time of worship with Don Moen. I had the privilege of baptizing her in the Jordan River. She shares how God moved on her during that trip and how He moved her forward on her path. Her story will encourage your faith.
Michael Coleman
Cofounder and former CEO of Integrity Music (1987-2011)
MikeColeman.com

LIVING WATERS

A Journey of Faith and Discovery
Connecting the Past with the Present

Judy Davis

Living Waters
Published by Quantum Shift Media
Denver, Colorado

Copyright © 2020 Judy Davis. All rights reserved.

ISBN: 978-0-9985303-4-5 (Paperback)
ISBN: 978-0-9985303-5-2 (Ebook)
Fourth Edition

Video still shots | Carol Trader Boone: p. 104, 107.
John Edwin Hobson: p. 108.

Title page art: "Scepter" by Janice VanCronkhite/JVCArtworks.com

Editing, cover, and book design | Quantum Shift Media

The Scripture quotations contained in this book are from The New King James Version, Copyright © 1982. Nashville: Thomas Nelson. *The New American Standard Bible*®, Copyright © 1960, 1962, 1963, 1971, 1972, 1973, 1975, 1977, 1995 by The Lockman Foundation. The Amplified Bible Old Testament copyright © 1965, 1987 by The Zondervan Corporation. The Amplified New Testament copyright © 1958, 1987 by The Lockman Foundation.

No part of this book may be reproduced in any form by any mechanical means, including information storage and retrieval systems without permission in writing from the publisher/author, except by a reviewer who may quote passages in a review.

All images in this book are subject to use according to trademark and copyright laws of the United States of America.

Contents

Dedication 12
Acknowledgments 13
Introduction 14
Prologue 15

Part I Blood Ancestry

Chapter 1 - America's Hidden Treasure 19
    Spiritual Heritage of the Huguenots 19
    America's First Marytrs 20
    Fort Caroline and the First Thanksgiving 20
    Cross This Line and You Die! 22
    A Line in the Sand 23
    The Redemptive Death of the Huguenots 24
    Passenger Manifest 24
    DNA 25

Chapter 2 - The Little Nightcap 27
    The Infamous Suzanne Rochet 27
    Setting the Stage: The Edict of Nantes 28
    The Revocation of the Edict of Nantes 28
    The Little Nightcap 30

Chapter 3 - Pocahontas 35
    The Delightful Matoaka 35
    Michaux, Rochet, and Pocahontas 35
    Pocahontas Sails to England 39

Chapter 4 - Paleo-Indian Ancestors 43
    Paleo-Indians and the Hebrew Script 43
    Paleo-Hebrew Script 45

Chapter 5 - Who Were The Huguenots? 49

CHAPTER 6 - THE REFORMATION 57
    JOHN CALVIN AND THE HUGUENOTS 57
    STUNNING DISCOVERY.. 58
    ELLIS ISLAND AND MY DNA 61
    DNA RESULTS: 61
    CONCLUSION 61

CHAPTER 7 - CONSTANTINE'S SWORD 63
    HISTORY OF THE HUGUENOTS UNDER CONSTANTINE 63
    THE ORIGINAL PRIMITIVES 63
    CONSTANTINE'S CULTURAL INFLUENCE TODAY 65
    THE FIRST COUNCIL OF NICEA 66

CHAPTER 8 - TAPESTRY OF SUFFERING 69
    THE CRUSADES 69
    ANTI-SEMITISM: 70
    THE APOSTLE PAUL TO THE ROMANS: 71

PART II REFLECTIONS

REFLECTIONS 74

CHAPTER 9 - A WALK BACK IN TIME 75
    THE TOBACCO FARM 75
    THE LION AND THE ROCK 77
    THE MOUNTAIN TOP 78
    PRIMITIVE BAPTISTS 79
    MARRIAGE 80
    THE DOCTRINE OF LIMITED ATONEMENT 81
    THE MORAVIANS 81
    THE MORAVIANS AND COUNT ZINZENDORF 83
    THE INTERVENTION 85
    ITS GLOWING 85
    GOD'S HEART — GOD'S FIRE 87

CHAPTER 10 - LIVING WATERS 89
    ANGEL IN MY CLOSET 89

CHAPTER 11 - QUENCHING THE SPIRIT.. 93
    THE VEIL THINS 93
    QUENCHING THE FIRE OF THE HOLY SPIRIT 93
    DISCERNMENT 94
    SAYING GOODBYE 97

PART III GRABBING THAT SWORD AGAIN

CHAPTER 12 - THE JOY OF THE LORD IS MY STRENGTH 99
    FINDING THE WELL... 99
    WEEPING FOR JOY... 100
    SUSAN MILLER 100
    VISION FOR ISRAEL - THE JOSEPH STOREHOUSE...................... 101
    STANDING IN THE GAP 103

CHAPTER 13 - HIS BANNER OVER ME IS LOVE 105
    MY MENTOR... 106
    JULIE ANN KIMBALL 109
    BANNERS IN THE PRISON 109
    GOD'S HEART; GOD'S PLAN 112
    JULIE'S SERVANTHOOD 114
    GOODBYE JULIE.. 115
    FATHER'S WAITING ARMS 117

PART IV MISSIONS: FROM JAMAICA TO AUSCHWITZ

CHAPTER 14 - JAMAICA SETS THE STAGE.................................... 123
    SEEING THE NEED FOR MISSIONS 123

CHAPTER 15 - MISSION TRIP TO ENGLAND 129
    HYDE PARK, 1998 129
    LONDON CITY MISSIONS... 130
    DOING IT AFRAID 132
    LEGAL GROUND 133
    HOSTILE PLACE.. 134
    LINZ, AUSTRIA... 137

CHAPTER 16 - REJECTION, REDEMPTION, AND THE
RIVER OF LIFE 139
   THE STORY OF HASSELL.. 139
   A WITNESS.. 143

CHAPTER 17 - JERUSALEM ARISE 145
   HOLY LAND PILGRIMAGE 145
   DIVINE APPOINTMENT AND A PRAISE REPORT 149
   ANGELS IN THE RAFTERS 150
   TOURING ISRAEL.. 151
   THE SPIRIT OF THE LORD SPEAKS 153

CHAPTER 18 - CHINA OUTREACH 155
   KEEP YOUR EYES DOWN.. 155
   LATE NIGHT MISSIONS.. 157
   TRACT TROUBLE AHEAD 158
   CINDY, OH CINDY!.. 161
   THE STRANGER.. 163
   CONNECTING THE DOTS 167

CHAPTER 19 - THE SEED PEARL 169
   ARABIC TAPES... 169
   THE VISION 172

CHAPTER 20 - DRAMA TEAM 175
   BOLIVIA AND QUITO, ECUADOR................................... 175

CHAPTER 21 - TWO MISSION TRIPS TO THE LAND 177
   THE JOSEPH STOREHOUSE... 178
   SHOUT TO THE NORTH AND SOUTH 183
   MISSION OF SOLIDARITY... 183
   MISSION IN HEBRON... 186
   THE ONE NEW MAN 188
   GOD'S HEART—GOD'S FIRE 190

CHAPTER 22 - MY TURKISH FRIEND................................... 191
   BOOK OF REVELATION TOUR... 191
   NEW REVELATIONS.. 192
   UNHAPPY CAMPER 193
   RIGHT ON CUE 193

PART V IDENTIFICATION REPENTANCE

- Chapter 23 - Auschwitz, Poland 199
  - Two Pages in a Book 200
  - Death Factories 201
  - Auschwitz and Sunflowers 202
  - Four Atrocities 203
  - The Wind of the Spirit 205
  - Blood Cries Out 207

- Chapter 24 - Remembering the Holocaust 211

- Chapter 25 - Rome and Generational Redemption 215
  - Accidental Confession 216
  - Our Calling to Rome 216
  - Blood Guilt and DNA 217
  - Bloodguilt 218
  - The Ceremony 219
  - The Vatican 219
  - Generational Redemption 220
  - Different Times, Different Seasons, Different Era 222

- Chapter 26 - Cleansing the Ground 223
  - For His Glory 224

- Epilogue 225
  - Wrapping It Up 225
  - The Hand Print 225

- Appendix 227
  - My DNA Result 227
  - The Davis Connection 228
  - The Michaux Data 228
  - Suzanne La Roche Rochet 229
  - The Michaux-Pocahontas Connection 234
  - Examining the Data Gained from the Huguenot Society ... 234

- About the Author 237

DEDICATION

To my Granddaughters,
Austyn Rose and Natalie Elizabeth

Acknowledgments

To Keren Kilgore of Quantum Shift Media, who worked so diligently and patiently to help me bring this book to its highest level of quality and excellence.

To Carrie Stiles, whose work as my research assistant was so vitally important.

I am grateful to my sister, Brenda, who hosted family gatherings in my place during holidays when my banner team was performing and for joining hands with me in love and support for Israel and the Jewish people. As my only sister, you are, and always have been, a blessing beyond measure.

To my cousin, Charlotte, who supplied the meticulous documents delineating our ancestry lines all the way back to Edward III of England.

And to my sons, Jesse and John, you are God's unique gift to me, my treasure in earthen vessels, the pride and joy of my life. To my daughter-in-law, Kathryn. You became part of the Davis family tree at just the right moment in our lives. What a blessing you are. And to my granddaughters, you light up my life in too many ways to count.

Lastly, to my Heavenly Father and His Holy Spirit for leading me on this incredibly rewarding journey at long last recorded.

Judy Davis

Introduction

Living Waters is a compilation of my life experiences, ancestral connections, historical truths and insights reflecting who I am in Christ and what God purposed my life to be. It was through my participation in missions that my intimacy with Him increased along with my faith. Whether I was cleaning the teeth of children in Jamaica, witnessing on the streets of London, smuggling Bibles into China, or participating in drama presentations on the streets of Ecuador and Bolivia, missions became a fundamental part of my life.

I did not purpose to dye silks, to outfit a dance team, or choreograph dance and banner presentations before local congregations and take them into a men's prison. Neither did I plan to research my ancestry eleven generations back in time. Yet, God purposed these things for me and when He did, I changed course to walk in the center of His will for me. Now that I am in my golden years, I look back through the curtain of time and see the tapestry of my life formed by the threads of my lineage. I hope that by sharing bits and pieces of it, the Holy Spirit will enlighten, encourage, and enhance all the ways in which He is working. And to God be the glory.

I chose a sunflower as the chapter heading in my book because it symbolizes faith, worship, spiritual knowledge, and a desire to seek light and truth.

Prologue

I am passionate about genealogical research. Looking into our roots helps us understand our own existence. We can use what we learn about ourselves and our past to influence our future. Our activities impact future generations just as the activities of our ancestors affected us physically and spiritually.

A chronology of my genealogy back through my family lineage to Pocahontas of America and the Huguenots of France reveals hidden threads of truth that led me to discover how God often moves when territories are reclaimed by ancestor association and acts of repentance on their behalf. The inclusion of my genealogy is a testimony to the power of invisible threads that connect us generationally, establishing the spiritual ground for kingdom work.

It is with this in mind that I have researched my ancestors' activities and the activities of others in history and recorded them in this book. At first, I did not think that my ancestors would have anything to do with my call to missions in diverse places of the world or that they would connect me to certain territories in the United States and abroad.

Ten generations have come and gone since the bloodline from a descendant of the Paleo Indian princess, Pocahontas, comingled with the DNA of the Huguenot, Joseph Michaux. And yet, one can clearly see from my memoirs how that connection impacted my spiritual journey. My journey took me to Holocaust Memorials on three continents and to a deeper understanding of the sufferings of the Moravian Christians, the martyrdom of Jan Hus, the persecution of my Huguenot ancestors, as well as the lasting negative effects of the Catholic-Protestant struggle. It also brought revelation regarding Constantine's influences upon those of the original faith who were Jewish disciples and 1st Century followers of Jesus.

Multiple layers of Constantinian influence still exist in Protestant and Catholic churches today, with Easter being a primary example. Constantine changed the original observance of Jesus' death and resurrection from the Jewish Feast of Passover to incorporate the pagan holiday celebrating the spring fertility rites of the ancient goddess, Ishtar.

In doing so, he moved the most sacred of Christian observances away from its Hebraic foundation of Jesus being our Passover Lamb.

Within the pages of this book, I have revealed the plight of my ancestors and the bloodshed that came from governments seeking religious and political control. With these things in mind, I write my memoirs knowing the terrible burdens some Christians face as they serve Him in diverse places of the world.

As I look back over the years, I am continually amazed at where God has led me, what He has brought me through, and what He has asked me to do for His kingdom despite my character flaws. It is my humble desire and a great privilege to share His overwhelming love, holiness, and acceptance. Instead of condemning me for my humanity, He met me at the place of my deepest need and set me down on the solid ground, and as He revealed His ongoing plan for my life, I never looked back.

It is my ultimate desire that the reader will seek out his or her own ancestral lineage and enjoy a greater understanding of family, traditions, and history.

*On the other side
Of the curtain of time
Threads woven in a
Tapestry I now call mine
Rivers of water flowing
From a God that is sewing
Threads of restoration
Mercy for the nations*

-Judy Davis

Part I

Blood Ancestry

Chapter 1

America's Hidden Treasure

*They overcame him by the blood of the Lamb,
and by the word of their testimony;
and they loved not their lives unto the death.*

Revelation 12:11 KJV

Spiritual Heritage of the Huguenots

Each of you is a living thread, delineated from bloodlines going back generations. They form the tapestry that is your life.

Two of my threads are noteworthy in that my sister and I are direct descendants of Suzanne Rochet, a French Huguenot, who fled France aboard a ship in a Hogshead to escape religious persecution in the 1600s, and the Indian princess, Pocahontas, daughter of the chief of the Powhatan Tribe of America's First Nations.

My story begins with the little known account of the first attempt at colonization of America (1564), which was not by the pilgrims at Plymouth Rock, but by French Huguenots who landed at what is now Jacksonville, Florida.

I will tell the story of America's First Thanksgiving at Fort Caroline, America's First Martyrs, and I will reveal the origin of the expression "a line in the sand."

America's First Marytrs

Sixty-six years before the Pilgrims who were seeking religious freedom arrived in Plymouth, Massachusetts, another group of settlers, known as the Huguenots, departed from France and arrived in modern-day Jacksonville, Florida. While the Pilgrims have become an important part of American culture, the Huguenot journey to Florida has become a forgotten part of American history.

After the many attempts to settle Florida by the Spanish, it was beginning to seem like a hopeless goal. But, as if on cue, after the failure of 1559, France, instead of Spain, had three ships on their way to Florida in February of 1562.

In the 16th Century, many in France began to embrace ideas of Reformation and break away from the teachings of Rome, choosing instead to study the Bible for themselves. The Catholic Church at that time (which was the official church of France) was greatly threatened by this move, which it interpreted as a weakening of its absolute authority over the people. As a result, the Huguenots were harassed continuously, and some even faced death rather than give up their faith.

By the middle of the 16th Century, some Huguenots, under the leadership of Gaspard de Coligny, Admiral of France, and prominent Huguenot, began to seek a way of escape from this persecuted lifestyle. In 1560, de Coligny (who was a man of great wealth) began to find favor in the court of nine-year-old King Charles IX and his influential mother, Catherine de Medici. He worked out a plan with the royal family that would allow the Huguenots to explore the New World and to eventually establish a colony there if the colonists would promise to search for the rumored silver and gold once they were there.[1]

Fort Caroline and the First Thanksgiving

French Admiral Gaspard de Coligny sent Admiral Jean Ribault to North America. He landed at the mouth of a river named "Mai" (the St. Johns River of Jacksonville) in the month of May. Ribault's

---

[1] *The Martyrs of Matanzas*, (2004). Published by Capitol Hill Prayer Partners, Herndon, VA, p. 3.

arrival also provided the first Protestant prayer offered up on North American soil. During his days on the river, the Native American Indians he encountered were friendly. He later sailed North and established a small settlement near present-day Port Royal, South Carolina, and returned to France. At that time, all of the southeastern United States was called Florida.

In 1564, one of Ribault's officers, Rene Laudonnière, was sent back from France with 300 men and four women. They built Fort Caroline six miles up the St. Johns River. Again, the Indians welcomed the returning Frenchmen who survived with the help of Timucuan Indians' grains, fruit, and wild game. With this apparent success, Laudonnière called for music and a feast on June 30, 1564, to celebrate their good fortune. Of this celebration, he wrote: "We sang a psalm of Thanksgiving unto God, beseeching Him that it would please His Grace to continue His accustomed goodness toward us." This was 57 years before the better known Thanksgiving celebration at Plymouth, Massachusetts. Laudonnière retrieved two Spanish sailors thought to have been shipwrecked with Fontaneda from the Indians in 1564.

The following year, Admiral Ribault sailed again with seven more ships to reinforce the French colony. Meanwhile, back in Catholic Spain, the news of the French Huguenots establishing a colony in Spanish Florida was not received well. To the Spanish, the Huguenots were Protestant Lutherans though they were followers of John Calvin. Spanish King Philip II reversed his position on not settling Florida, and Pedro Menendez de Aviles was sent to the same area to destroy the "heretical" Frenchmen.

Menendez arrived shortly after the French ships of Ribault with Spain's largest force yet: 1,504 men in 19 ships. The French were not expecting a naval battle, so Menendez chose to challenge the French immediately. Not prepared to do battle, Admiral Ribault immediately got under sail, but a storm wrecked his fleet at sea. Menendez then chose not to attack, sailed south to St. Augustine, and marched back over the land to capture the French at Fort Caroline, taking them completely by surprise. He renamed it San Mateo, which is now Jacksonville.

At Fort Caroline, about 60 women and children were spared. Laudonnière and 40 or 50 others managed to escape and went back to France.[2]

Cross This Line and You Die!

Menendez returned to St. Augustine pleased with his efforts at Fort Caroline but not yet fully satisfied with his mission. His primary goal had yet to be achieved: to find and kill Jean Ribault, the leader of the Huguenot community. Now aware that Ribault and 300 of his men had sailed southward down the coast, Menendez's next step was clear: continue to search until those men were found and dealt with.

Soon after they had left Fort Caroline, Ribault's men (who were sailing in three ships) encountered the same storm that had been raging at Fort Caroline. This ferocious hurricane was huge, howling for days up and down the Florida coast. After battling this storm for several days, all three ships were eventually destroyed in the ocean waters. As the men swam to safety on the shore, they ended up stranded on a strip of sand about fifteen miles south of St. Augustine where they waited for help while they tried to evade Menendez's search party.

On September 27, Captain Menendez got the news he was waiting for from local Indians: Ribault and his men had been shipwrecked to the south and were marching up the coast, almost 500 men in two groups, toward Fort Caroline. Menendez then set out with 50 of his men to find and get rid of them. Two days later, on September 29, the Spanish met the first group of French Huguenots on the sands of Matanzas, which means "slaughters." It was there that this group had stopped, unable to traverse the deep, running waters of this inlet.

---

[2]Wilkinson, J. (n.d.). "Influence of France on Florida." An article on general history of the French presence, 1562-1763. Retrieved from http://www.keyshistory.org/FL-Fla-Fr.html.

A Line in the Sand

Quoting from literature provided by the National Park Service:

Famished and weary, informed of their fort's capture, and tricked into believing the Spanish force to be much larger, the French surrendered. On September 29, they were ferried ten at a time across the inlet, fed, and led behind the dunes, where their hands were bound. About 200 feet down the beach, Menendez drew a line in the sand. At the line, Menendez gave each man an opportunity to renounce Protestantism (called the "new religion") and live, or cross the line and meet his Maker. On that day, 111 Christian men were martyred; Menendez spared only those who stated that they were of the Catholic faith, and those who played the flute, timbrel and harp. The total number of survivors was 16. Even with these two slaughters behind him, Menendez still was not satisfied, because Jean Ribault was still alive somewhere yet on the Florida coast.

Again, quoting the Park Service:

Twelve days later, Menendez heard that the second group of 350 Frenchmen had likewise halted at the inlet. Again there was a parley - this time with Ribault himself, who saw the gruesome evidence of the first massacre. [The others had been run through with pike, dagger, and sword.] Ribault returned and told his men everything. He advised surrender, for he believed, it appeared that the Spaniards would show mercy. But during the night more than half of his men fled south. The next morning, October 12, Ribault and his remaining men handed their battle flags to Menendez.

As before, the Huguenots were brought in groups of ten across the water and again the white sands were darkened with blood. That day, 134 Frenchmen lost their lives; 16 were spared.

Later, Menendez sought out those who had fled; most he took to Habana as prisoners.[3]

---

[3]Ballenger, S., Burk, A., Corley, L. (2004). America's Buried Treasure, The Martyrs of Matanzas, Published by Capital Hill Prayer Partners, Herndon, Va. pp. 9-10.

Fort Matanzas was designated as a National Monument by President Calvin Coolidge on October 15, 1924. It marks the spot where 500 French Colonists were slaughtered by the Spanish in 1565. Pedro Menendez gave a name to this river inlet: "Matanzas," meaning slaughters. The island itself, now called Rattlesnake Island, was then called Basilisk.

The Redemptive Death of the Huguenots

I call it *legal ground*. For when that line in the sand was drawn, the Lord Himself drew a line in the sand against the devil's attempt to keep America from becoming *one nation under God*.

> *God's ultimate destiny and purpose for this nation is to function as one nation under God and to release the gospel to the uttermost parts of the earth. It will be fulfilled. No weapon against it will prosper because of this blood soaked line in the sand. This is "America's hidden treasure."*[4]

Passenger Manifest

Among the list of passengers on board ship that landed at Fort Caroline (from Florida's Park Service), I found the surname of *La Roche-Ferrere* among the list of passengers. My Huguenot ancestor, Suzanne Rochet, holds the same surname. According to the Powhatan County Historical Society, Suzanne Rochet's entire given name is Suzanne Laroche Rochet. This indicates to me that Laroche was a family surname as well.

Just as amazing to me is the name Ferrere attached to LaRoache on the passenger manifest. It was a French Huguenot by the name of Armond La-Ferrere, who wrote the essay *The Huguenots, the Jews and*

---

[4]Excerpt from "America's Buried Treasure," Capital Hill Prayer Partners, Herndon, Va., June 30, 2004. pp. 1

Me[5] (See Chapter Six: The Theology of the Huguenots) supplying a vital link to the Hebraic mindset of my Huguenot ancestors. His article and subsequent essay provided information fueling the flame already burning in my heart to learn more about my roots. It was Armand LaFerrere who questioned his own mysterious, Huguenot family's Philo-Semitism, their Hebraic mindset, and love for Israel and the Jewish people.

DNA

Could it be that the same DNA in a passenger willing to risk his life to escape religious persecution and colonize America has a genetic link to my ancestor who escaped France aboard a ship for the same reason?

The Sands of Time

Hidden threads once concealed
Hidden Threads now revealed
From the Tapestry of time
Threads begin to shine
Giving forth light of a kind
That binds this history to mine

-Judy Davis

---

[5]Laferrere, A. (2006). "The Huguenots, the Jews, and Me: A Tale of French Philo-Semitism." Shalem Press: AzureOnline, Autumn 5767 / 2006, no. 26. Retrieved from http://azure.org.il/article.php?id=43. The original article in its entirety was removed from the internet after Laferrere's death in 2013, but portions of it can still be found by looking for "The Huguenots, The Jews and Me by Armand Laferrere."

CHAPTER 2

THE LITTLE NIGHTCAP

The Infamous Suzanne Rochet

She had never been so frightened in her 18 years. She was sealed in a wine cask, had been for 16 hours. It was suffocating, damp, and foul from her own body's natural functions. She could hear very little, because the inside of the cask was padded thickly with pillows. Air could get in only through a narrow crack near the bottom. She stifled a scream when a hard thumping hit the side of the barrel. She realized that the French gendarmes were hitting the barrel with their rifle butts to make sure no one was hidden within. Then all was quiet and there was a sense of being suspended—she knew she was being lowered into the hole of the Englishman's ship. Total dark, damp, cold, and only the sound of scurrying rats as the ship put out to sea from France.[6]

---

[6]Tucker, C. (2008). The Powhatan County Historical Society. "The Huguenots' Search for Religious Freedom: America's Gain." Retrieved from www.powhatanhistoricalsociety.org/cemetery/hist-talk-1.html.

Setting the Stage: The Edict of Nantes

The Edict of Nantes was formed in 1598 in response to the Wars of Religion (1562-1598)[7] under Henry III, father of Edward II, who succeeded Charles IX. The Huguenots, led by Henry of Navarre, defeated the Catholics in 1587 at Coutras. Catholic infighting caused the deaths of the Duc de Guise in 1588 and Henry III in 1589. With these strong Catholic leaders gone, *Protestant Henry of Navarre* became the first monarch of the Bourbon line as King. To keep the peace, he converted to Catholicism in 1593. Five years later, he issued the *Edict of Nantes* granting almost complete religious freedom to the Protestants. As a result, the Protestants embraced their hard-won freedom and thrived as the religious wars ended. His Edict identified 20 safe cities in France where the Huguenots could practice their faith. Unfortunately, Henry (now referred to as Henry the IV) was murdered by a Catholic monk and peace ended for the protestants.

His grandson, Louis XIV desired absolute power and had no tolerance for the Protestants. He believed religious diversity would weaken his kingdom politically, so he decided to bring all of France under one common religion: Catholicism. His revocation of the Edict was deemed one of the greatest acts of religious intolerance in history.

The Revocation of the Edict of Nantes

The revocation in 1685 brought riotous persecutions. Overnight, all children became illegitimate because the church no longer recognized marriages between Protestants. This left property and inheritances vulnerable for confiscation. Affected Huguenots fled for Holland, Switzerland, the Netherlands, Germany, and England while others left the continent for the English colonies in America.

---

[7]Retrieved from http://www.britannica.com/EBchecked/topic/497152/Wars-of-Religion.

The move resulted in the complete destruction of Protestant gathering areas, and schools. In addition, no form of Protestant worship was to take place in private. Anyone not willing to convert had to leave France without their property within two weeks of the new Edict. However, no children would be allowed to leave; they would have to remain in France and convert to Catholicism. Newborns were to be baptized Catholic and could not emigrate. Those who had already left could return within four months without penalty if they renounced their Protestantism and converted to Catholicism. (Perhaps that is why my ancestors did not leave—they had children.)

Protestants were removed from office, denied their normal living, stripped of their possessions, and faced near extinction. Forced conversions required the Huguenots to take the host (bread and wine) as the literal body and blood of Christ and Protestants who spit it out were reportedly tortured by burning. Parisian Protestant nobles were incarcerated in the Bastille under harsh conditions. They were not tortured but remained there until they converted to Catholicism or died. The Huguenots saw their individual salvation as a reflection of God's relationship with the Jews and secretly engaged in the primitive worship rites of their Jewish ancestors. These rituals were threatened by the Huguenot's own children who were taught to watch for illegal Protestant practices and inadvertently turned them in through innocent statements. The fact that the Huguenot preachers knew and spoke Hebrew would be an indication that the Huguenots were practicing the forbidden religion of the Jews. *(Remember that Constantine made it illegal for Messianic Jews to worship on the Sabbath or observe the Feast of Passover as well as other feasts.)* Speaking Hebrew was a red flag and a clear sign of an illegal practice.

Since Louis XIV wished to keep the industrious Huguenots in France because they were excellent for the economy and had considerable wealth, he discouraged emigration and encouraged forced conversions to Roman Catholicism, especially of their children. When he ordered them out of the mountainous region of Camisard in France more than 15 years after the revocation of the Edict of Nantes, nearly half a million French Huguenots again fled France.

Those who settled in the Netherlands dug in and prospered, and eventually became the very people responsible for defending the Netherlands against Louis XIV and for returning James II to the English throne.

The Little Nightcap

It was amidst these tumultuous times that my ancestor, Suzanne Laroche Rochet (1667-1744), was born in Sedan (Cedent), France. Years later, after the revocation of the Edict of Nantes, her father, Moses Rochet, sent his children to Holland to save them from the forced conversion to Roman Catholicism. He was able to pay a tax or ransom for the right to remain in France as a Protestant with his wife since he was a wealthy man but not so his children. Huguenot children were declared illegitimate and in danger of being taken and raised by Nuns. The account of his children's escape to Holland is told in the story "The Little Nightcap" and several historical accounts. I have chosen the one account written by a descendant of Suzanne Rochet (M'me Patty Venable)[8] in William Henry Foote's book because it gives the same account I was given by my mother and my great-grandfather, Richard Randolph Michaux in his book *Sketches of Life in North Carolina*.[9]

According to the report by William Foote, Suzanne was the youngest daughter of the Rochets at the time of the revocation of the Edict of Nantes. Moses Rochet's eldest daughter, Jeanne, was 18 years old by the time she had been examined three times by Roman priests or government officials.

---

[8]Foote, W. H. (1870). *The Huguenots: Or, Reformed French Church. Their Principles Delineated; Their Character Illustrated, Their Sufferings and Success Recorded*, Richmond: Presbyterian Committee of Publication. p. 541. Retrieved from http://www.unz.org/Pub/FooteWilliam-1870.

[9]Michaux, R. (1823-1899). *Sketches of Life in North Carolina: Embracing Incidents and Narratives, and Personal Adventures of the Author During Forty Years of Travel in 1894.*

The Little Nightcap

Foote reports that as a result of the increasing dangers in the area, Moses Rochet sent Jeanne away with a niece (not a sister) who had an infant child. The two were accompanied to the seaport to catch a ship to Holland by men dressed as women, called nightwalkers. Huguenots are sometimes defined as those who walk at night.

That night, the infant cried when the mother stumbled on some rocks while they were crossing a mill stream, and the soldiers guarding the place were roused. The young women were apprehended and sent to prison.

Moses Rochet was able to gain back his daughter while her cousin was retained as an example to other potential escapees and marched about in public to endure the ridicule of onlookers. As to the fate of the infant, there is no record, but the account shows the niece's husband had already gone ahead to Holland seeking employment as a carpenter. There is no record that Moses was able to retrieve his niece. However, there is some evidence he was able to gain her freedom because he "paid various sums of money to obtain peace," indicating more than one transaction, and "he made an attempt to send his two elder daughters to Holland."[10]

As the storyline goes in M'me Venable's account, the two sisters wrote their father to send them the little nightcap left behind when they left Sedan, and many reports say that this code referring to Suzanne made her the youngest of three sisters instead of two sisters. And here, the account presents an error as evidenced in Foote's book.

Since it was Jeanne who was under scrutiny by the authorities, Moses may have felt it necessary to get her out of France. Since the niece's husband was already settled in Amsterdam, perhaps he sent these two girls ahead, keeping Suzanne with him (her father).

After combining the resources from all of those available at the time of this writing (birth and baptism records), I know that Moses Rochet had only two daughters, Suzanne and Jeanne. They were born two years apart, and the girls were aged 18 and 20 in 1685. Moses Rochet's niece attempted to make the trip the first time with Jeanne, and Moses may have been able to get her out of prison for another

---

[10] Foote, W.H. (1870). The Huguenots or Reformed French Church. Richmond, VA. P. 543. Retrieved from http://www.archive.org/stream/huguenotsorrefor00foot.

flight. It had to have been this niece and Jeanne who fled the country with Suzanne following in the hogshead cask. The various versions and discrepancies of the story may have occurred due to the code "little nightcap." Being a code, it follows that it does not necessarily mean Suzanne was a "little girl" at the time of her escape in the hogshead. Whiskey casks are known as a hogshead afforded room for a small adult. Then too, adding to the confusion is the report that Suzanne's "two sisters" married men and moved to the West Indies.

A hogshead for dry goods during colonial times

Suzanne stayed in Holland, married Abraham Michaux, also a refugee from Sedan, France, on July 13, 1692. They had four children (baptized at the French Church of Amsterdam, as Anne, Jean, Issac and Jacques before moving to England and immigrating to America.) These two sisters who married and moved to the West Indies were likely Jeanne and her cousin since Suzanne only had one sister.

Just at the turn of the Century, King William offered "encouragement" in the form of lands and compensation to anyone willing to settle in the new colonies in Virginia, and the couple traveled to Stafford County with their six children reaching the banks of the Potomac River around 1702. They joined the colony on the James River within two years of their arrival. Their oldest son, Issac (Jacob), struck out alone and settled on the James River in an area known as Michaux's Ferry.

> Jane Magdalene Michaux
> Ester Mary Michaux
> Anne Madeline "Nannie" Michaux
> Issac "Jacob" Michaux
> Susannah Rochet Michaux
> Olive Judith Michaux
> Elizabeth Michaux

The Little Nightcap

Jacques (John) Michaux
Abraham Michaux
Jean Paul Michaux

According to an article in the Richmond Times Dispatch, the English and American records say that Suzanne and Abraham came to the colonies sometime between August 1702 and November 1705. They are reported to have first settled in Stafford County, Virginia after receiving their land grant from King William. They moved to a Huguenot settlement known as Manakintowne in 1705. There, Abraham Michaux received a patent which is a land-grant of 574 acres on the south side of the James River but sold it in 1707. In 1713, he obtained another patent for 850 acres plus an additional deed (land grant) on 230 acres in 1715 from King William's successor, King George I, who took the throne in 1714.

Today, the "Michaux Grant" estate is located near Richmond, Virginia in Jamestown. The Michaux Bridge over the James River is named in honor of them. The remains of the Michaux family home can still be seen near Richmond. A fire destroyed most of it, but one section still stands as part of the new estate.

CHAPTER 3

POCAHONTAS

The Delightful Matoaka

I learned of my colorful ancestry from my mother, whose ancestors had kept meticulous records of their genealogy, which was vital to researching my own; hence, my ancestry can be traced back ten generations directly to Pocahontas whose bloodline is uniquely connected to the French Huguenots through Joseph Michaux.

When I began looking at my family genealogy and discovered the Pocahontas–Rolfe connection to the Michaux name, I realized that this early American/Native American bloodline had co-mingled with Huguenot blood back with the entrance of Joseph Michaux into the family line through his marriage to Anne Meade Randolph. The bloodline of Anne Meade Randolph (daughter of cousins Ann and Brett Randolph, Jr.) can be traced back to Edward III, King of England, who reigned from 1327 to 1377, the year of his death.

Michaux, Rochet, and Pocahontas

Historical records containing the surnames of my ancestors, Michaux and Rochet, are meticulously maintained by the National Huguenot Society, the Huguenot Society of Virginia, and others. Although the family names on record vary according to the accepted spellings by region, I have settled on the version recorded by my

Living Waters

1616 | Portrait of Pocahontas

ancestors Michaux and Rochet (pronounced *Ro-chay*) from my mother's lineage. The Michaux name can be traced back to Pocahontas (1595-1617) through a Michaux marriage to a Randolph.

Pocahontas means "bright stream between two hills" and "playful one." Her given name was Matoaka, which means snow feather. According to historians, Pocahontas was a pet name given to her by her father, Powhatan, since it was a tradition in the Tsenacommacah tribal region for natives to give secret names to loved ones. Another reason for hiding the birth name was to protect loved ones from spirits or persons who might wish them harm.

History records how Pocahontas saved Captain John Smith's life in 1607 when the 12-year-old prevented her father from bludgeoning Smith to death. It is uncertain whether this was a benign tribal ritual or whether Smith was really in danger. However, most historians support the latter explanation, and Smith recorded in later years that Pocahontas saved him from being whacked on the head with a tomahawk. John Smith referenced this event in a letter to Queen Anne in 1616 and again in 1627 in his memoirs. Other references record that he may have written about his encounters with Pocahontas as early as 1608.

It was on account of Pocahontas that the English supported the colonies with money and supplies. Smith reported that Pocahontas brought his colony food and provisions every few days, which helped keep these colonists alive and free from the fate of the legendary "Lost Colony" of Roanoke Island, North Carolina. The mysterious disappearance of America's Lost Colony was popularized by Paul Greene's long-running outdoor drama of said name and is still performed each summer in Manteo on Roanoke Island. The actor, Andy Griffith appeared more than once in the play and lived on the island until his death in 2012.

Pocahontas appears to have been enamored with Smith but would have been too young to be his actual lover. Additional evidence given for this assumption is the fact that after he was injured in a gunpowder accident in 1609 and returned to England for treatment, Pocahontas stopped visiting Jamestown, believing a rumor that he was dead. She abandoned the colony, lending credence to the supposition that Smith was the main reason she visited.

A painting of Pocahontas receiving her baptism
hanging in our nation's Capital building

In 1613, English Captain Samuel Argall took Pocahontas hostage, hoping to use her to negotiate a peace treaty with her father, Chief Powhatan. He brought her to Jamestown, and she was put under the custody of Sir Thomas Gates, the marshal of Virginia.

Gates treated her as a guest rather than a prisoner and encouraged her to learn English customs. She converted to Christianity and was baptized, Lady Rebecca. Powhatan eventually agreed to the terms for her release, but by then, she had fallen in love with John Rolfe, who was about ten years her senior. On April 5, 1614, Pocahontas and John Rolfe married with the blessing of Chief Powhatan and the governor of Virginia.[11]

The nuptials were documented in a letter written by Sir Thomas Dale, governor of Virginia, from Jamestown in June 1614. John Rolfe's letter to Sir Thomas Dale, the deputy governor of the colony, asked him to approve of his marriage to Princess Pocahontas. Rolfe attempted to explain why he, a devout Christian, desired to marry Pocahontas. He believed that his marriage was good for the colony and that he would be able to further the spread of Christian ideals through his role in Pocahontas' conversion. Rolfe also conveyed that he and Pocahontas loved each other and that their union would not compromise his standing in the colony or the Church. He wrote of his love for her in his letter to Dale, "To whom my hartie and best thoughts are, and have so long bin entangled and enthralled in so intricate a labyrinth that I was even aweared to unwind myself thereout."

The letter was first published in Ralph Hamor's tract "A True Discourse of the Present Estate of Virginia and the Successe of the Affaires There Till the 18 of June 1614" (London, 1615).[12] Chief Powhatan not only assented to the marriage but offered peace to the English settlers. The ensuing Peace of Pocahontas, which lasted eight years, allowed the English to grow and prosper and get enough settlers into Virginia that the Indians couldn't later kick them out.[13]

---

[11] This Day in History. Retrieved from http://www.history.com/this-day-in-history/pocahontas-marries-john-rolfe.

[12] Tyler, L.G. (editor), (1907). Narratives of Early Virginia, 1606-1625. New York: Charles Scribner's Sons.

[13] Author Unknown (April 5, 2013). "America's First Entrepreneur. Retrieved from http://americasfirstentrepreneur.com/tag/pocahontas.

Pocahontas Sails to England

In 1615, Pocahontas gave birth to a son, Thomas, and in 1616, the couple sailed to England. The Indian Princess proved popular with the English gentry, and she was presented at the court of King James I.[14] Once in England, Pocahontas was surprised to learn that Captain Smith was alive after having grieved his death so many years before. Upon seeing him, she was speechless and hid her face. Conflicting accounts exist of her reaction upon seeing him. It is reported that she was overcome either with anger that she had been lied to about his demise or for joy in seeing her friend. However, evidence shows that she at least spoke to him and may have even spent some time with him because Smith wrote that she called him "father."

She met King James in January of 1617, and two months later, boarded a ship bound for Virginia and home. Almost immediately, she became gravely ill, and the ship returned to England. After being put ashore, Pocahontas died in her husband's arms. She was only 22 years old and was buried in Gravesend, England. Her young son, Thomas, also took ill but recovered.[15] Rolfe returned to Virginia alone, leaving their only child in the care of his brother, Henry. Thomas Rolfe remained with his uncle until he was 20 years old (1635), at which time he sailed for Virginia. However, he never saw his father again as John Rolfe died suddenly in 1622 after a massacre when his tobacco plantation was destroyed. It is unsure whether he died of complications arising from the massacre or some other issue. His death left Thomas the family estate and lands. Thomas also inherited thousands of acres of land from his grandfather, Chief Powhatan, after his death in 1618. When Thomas met his Native American uncle, Opechancanough, who had taken over the tribes after Chief Powhatan's death, Thomas was forced to choose between his English and Native American heritage. He chose to remain an Englishman, no doubt, due to his upbringing.

---

[14]Retrieved from http://www.history.com/this-day-in-history/pocahontas-marries-john-rolfe.

[15]National Park Service (n.d.), Historic Jamestown: John Rolfe. Retrieved from http://www.nps.gov/jame/historyculture/thomas-rolfe.htm.

Living Waters

Pocahontas is significant in history largely because she befriended the colonists, was independent, outspoken, and courageous. She was the catalyst to gain English support for the new territory. Much was written about her vibrant personality and her favored status as the daughter of the chief. John Rolfe is often overlooked by historians in favor of the more exciting accounts of his colorful wife. However, the colony owes part of its survival to this tobacco merchant. He left England to invest his efforts and wealth in the colony and did as much to prosper the area as any man could. More than once, the colony found itself starving and in absolute despair, and Rolfe did as much to save it as his wife—Rolfe through the provision of industry and Pocahontas, while she was still a young girl, in bringing the provisions they needed for survival.

According to Wyndham Robertson, the name "Rolfe" is traced to the Vikings and the Danish all the way back to Rolf Krake, King of Denmark, in AD 600.[16] John Rolfe was a twin, born to John Rolfe and Dorothea Mason on May 6th, 1585. Once back at the colony, Rolfe married Jane Pierce in 1619, two years after Pocahontas's death. John Rolfe died shortly thereafter.

His son, Thomas Rolfe, returned to his birthplace in Virginia and there enjoyed the endowment of 400 acres of land at Fort James, also known as Chickahominy Fort, along with the houses and boats there on the property. His wife's name was Jane Poythress (also Poyers). His only child, Jane Rolfe, married Colonel Robert Bolling (1646-1709) in 1675 and died one year later shortly after having given birth to a son, John Bolling Jr. (1676-1729). See Appendix for complete history (Michaux Data) pertaining to the information below.

John was a member of the House of Burgess and married my ancestor, Mary Kennon. Tracing their line of descent:
- Anne Meade Randolph, daughter of Brett and Ann Randolph, married Joseph Michaux. Their union created the seventh line of descent from Pocahontas to my mother, making Pocahontas my 11th great grandmother.

---

[16] Robertson, W. (1887). *Pocahontas, Alias Matoaka, And Her Descendants Through Her Marriage At Jamestown, VA, in April, 1614.* J.W. Randolph & English: Richmond, VA. p. 27. Retrieved from https://archive.org/details/pocahontasalias00brocgoog.

- Ann Meade Randolph and Joseph Michaux produced three children, Richard Randolph, John, and Daniel.
- *Richard Randolph Michaux* (1823-1899), who in 1894, wrote "Sketches of Life in North Carolina: Embracing Incidents and Narratives of the Author During 40 Years of Travel," was married to *Anna Davis* who passed away after bearing him three children—Anna, Richard Jr. (who died in infancy), and John. He then married *Sallie Davis*, his wife's sister (my great-grandmother), and had William, Martha Rochet, Brett, *Mabel Claire*, Lucile Duty, and Sallie Garnet.
- *Mabel Clare Michaux* married *Luther Waugh McKinney* and bore him Lillian Lucille, Brett Dilworth, *Frances Michaux*, Mary Meade, and Laura Ruth.
- *Frances Michaux McKinney b. 1923 -d. 2001*, married *William Vester (Dock) Marshall b. 1917-d. 1995* and bore two children, *Brenda Caron b. 1942* and *Judy Gail b. 1944*. *Brenda Caron Marshall* married *Douglas R. McKinney* in 1961 and *Judy Gail Marshall* married *Jesse Shumate Davis, Jr.* in 1967.

And there you have my ancestry back to Pocahontas, a most colorful figure in American history, of whom I am quite happy and proud to share blood lineage.

Chapter 4

Paleo-Indian Ancestors

Paleo-Indians and the Hebrew Script

The Huguenot Society of the Founders of Manakin in the Colony of Virginia was organized on April 17, 1922, in memory of the French Protestant refugees who settled at Manakintown and in the Colony of Virginia prior to 1786. The aims of the Society are:[17]

To promote interest in the study of the Huguenots who settled Manakin and the lines descended therefrom.

To erect a lasting memorial at Manakintown in memory of its valiant settlers.

To collect all existing documents relating to Manakin and the Manakin Huguenots to be placed in a library for the use of the Society.

To encourage the preparation of fully documented papers and essays on the Manakin Huguenots and their ancestry for deposit in the Society Library and for publication in "The Huguenot" Magazine when space permits.

---

[17] The Huguenot Society of the Founders of Manakin in the Colony of Virginia (n.d.). "History of Virginia Huguenots and the Society." Retrieved from www.huguenot-manakin.org.

To sponsor Huguenot Memorials for the training of young people in intellectual and spiritual growth and development.

"The Society refers to the Monacan Indians in Manakintowne as Paleo-Indians. Monacans are reportedly part of the Powhatan Confederacy of tribes, the chief of which is none other than Pocahontas's father."[18] These tribes did not view their territorial boundaries as theirs in the same sense of ownership as the English and other Europeans since they believed only God owned the earth. However, by establishing boundaries and living within them, they owned the land for all intents and purposes until they were driven off by the American colonists.

The Native American Indians were able to adapt to the river's predictable seasonal ebbs and flows while white settlers struggled against them, and this river ran between two hills, which can be seen metaphorically as two nations—the Huguenot colony and the Monacan Indian Tribe (First Nations Indians).

Interestingly, the article "In River Time: The Way of the James" refers to land "high between two marshes, where John Smith counted 340 Native American inhabitants about two miles up Powell Creek south of Hopewell in the tidewater estuary." It is here that the land was never mined and where water levels were never high enough to erode its banks.[19] Because of this, archaeologists have been able to uncover bones and other treasures of this lost Paleo-Indian tribe known as the Weyanoke. *This land between two marshes lying within the township of Hopewell, Virginia, is where 2000-year-old pottery has been found.*

---

[18] The Huguenot Society of the Founders of Manakin in the Colony of Virginia (n.d.). "The Monacan Indians and Manakintown." Retrieved from http://huguenot-manakin.org/manakin/monacan.php.

[19] Author unknown (n.d.) In River Time: The Way of the James. "Primitive Legacies" retrieved from http://www.vcu.edu/engweb/Rivertime/chp3.htm.

Paleo-Hebrew Script

Looking at the ancient Paleo hieroglyphs found in North America, we can see the letters used on some of the rocks that clearly resemble ancient Hebrew letters. The picture below is of the Los Lunas Decalogue Stone found in New Mexico in 1997 on which a condensed version of the Ten Commandments is written.

Decaloque Stone found in 1997

Perhaps we can conclude from these fragments of evidence that the scattering of the Jewish people from their Holy Lands included certain tribes of the American Indians. From articles on Paleo-Hebrew about a lost Jewish script, a connection can be established, showing linkage to the script carved into the rock to the lost Hebrew alphabet.

There is one Hebrew language, but it has two different scripts. One of these scripts fell into complete disuse and was forgotten 2,000 years ago. Within the past century, it has been rediscovered. The impact of this discovery has not yet been fully felt for the lost script may well be the original, the one in which the Ten Commandments were written by the finger of God and the one in which Moses wrote the original Torah.

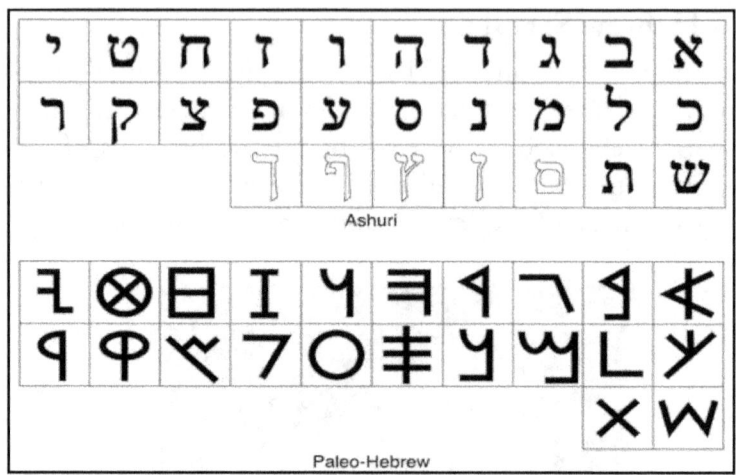

The lost script is called Ivri or Paleo-Hebrew. Our familiar Hebrew script is known as Ashuri or Assyrian script.

Paleo-Hebrew was completely abandoned around the time of the destruction of the second temple in the year 70 CE [Common Era] Except for the inscriptions on a few ancient Jewish coins, no remnant of Paleo-Hebrew remained. The Babylonian Talmud (Sanhedrin 21b) has a pertinent discussion about these two forms of Hebrew writing:

> *Mar Zutra[20] or, some say, Mar Ukba said: Originally the Torah was given to Israel in Ivri (Paleo-Hebrew) letters and in the sacred Hebrew language. Later, in the times of Ezra,[21] the Torah was given in Ashuri script and Aramaic language. Finally, they selected for Israel the Ashuri script and Hebrew language, leaving the original Hebrew[22] characters and Aramaic language for the ignorant people.*

---

[20]He passed away circa 414 C.E. Mar Zutra was a pious leader (Reish Galuta or Exilarch) of the Jewish community in Babylon. His opinions are cited frequently in the Talmud. Retrieved from http://www.jewishmag.com/160mag/original_hebrew_script/original_hebrew_script.html.

[21]Ezra the Scribe, generally acknowledged as the leader of the generation towards the end of the Babylonian Exile. Retrieved from http://www.jewishmag.com/160mag/original_hebrew_script/original_hebrew_script.html.

[22]Paleo-Hebrew or Ivri.

Rebbe Yose said: "Why is it called Ashuri (Assyrian) script? Because they brought it with them from Assyria." [23]

When the Jews returned to Israel to build the second temple, they brought this script with them from Babylon, here referred to as Assyria, as it is similarly called in Jeremiah 2:18 and Ezra 6:22. Today, northern Iraq comprises the ancient land of Assyria, and southern Iraq is Babylon. For more information, I highly recommend the article "The Gomez House: The Oldest Jewish Residence in the USA" by Samuel Kurinski.[24] In the early years of the evolution of the American nation, Jewish fur traders were among the first who ventured into the wilderness. These hardy pioneers established and maintained a friendly relationship with the Indian tribes. The continuity of their enterprise depended not only on a fair and mutually beneficial association between themselves and the Indians but on the continuing freedom of the Indians to live and hunt on their ancestral lands. At that early time, the possibility that the Indians were descended from the ten lost tribes of Israel was seriously discussed and considered in the Sephardic community of New York. Similarities between the religious rites of the two cultures and language peculiarities were taken as evidence that, indeed, a relationship existed which could not be ascribed to coincidence.

Some Rabbis insisted that Indians be dealt with as fellow Jews. It was argued that neither Hebrew nor the Indian languages make use of a comparative or superlative degree. It was noted that both languages make considerable use of hyperbole and metaphor. While such language parallels were not in themselves significant, they reinforced other cultural parallels of greater import.

It was said that the Indians worshiped a great spirit they called Yohovah. Indian holy days came about in the spring and the fall, corresponding to the Jewish Passover and Succoth. The Indians

---

[23]Retrieved from http://www.jewishmag.com/160mag/original_hebrew_script/original_hebrew_script.html.

[24]Kurinski, S. (n.d.). Hebrew History Federation. "Gomez House-The Oldest Jewish Residence in the USA" Fact Paper 30. Retrieved from www.hebrewhistory.info/factpapers/fp030_gomez.html.

underwent a two-day fast period, much as the Jews did on the Day of Atonement. It was observed that Indians had high priests, and one of their functions was the conduct of puberty rites. The Indians' sense of purity both in personal terms and in their diet was emphasized particularly because the Indians considered the eating of certain animals taboo. Finally, similarities between the Indian and the ancient Hebrew counting systems and the fact that the Indians employed a lunar calendar convinced many that, indeed, the two peoples were related.

Traditional lore has the Paleo-Indians crossing over a frozen landmass over the Bering Strait called Beringia that separates Russia from Alaska in search of better hunting grounds. They may have arrived as early as 50,000 BC. DNA research has determined that 95% of these groups are traceable to Asian peoples. However, 5% is not traceable to this ethnicity and stands unique in their blood lineage. Some think they may be part of the lost tribes of Israel arriving centuries later.

In a private conversation with Jesse Running Bear of North Carolina, I found out that at least ten Indian songs known and sung by a prominent old tribesman include the word Yahweh, which is the Hebrew name for the God of Israel.

Yah is a shortened version of the Hebrew God of Israel and can be found in scripture verses denoting psalms of ascent. "Oh Yah, Let God Arise" sung by Paul Wilbur during his concert "Jerusalem Arise" and DVD, was the first time I ever heard His (God's) "pet name" known to the Jews as being in the book of Psalms.

Given the strong spiritual nature of the American Indians, it could be that during the Assyrian conquests the ten lost tribes of Israel were carried away or traveled to foreign lands in keeping with Isaiah 27:6, "In the days to come, Jacob will put out shoots, Israel will bud and blossom and fill the whole world with fruit."

Excerpts from a multi-volume 19th Century work by British scholar Lord Kingsborough, *Antiquities of Mexico*,[25] show very strong evidence of this possibility.

---

[25] Antiquities of Mexico. Retrieved from http://www.youtube.com/watch?v=QorNrqDjcW0

CHAPTER 5

WHO WERE THE HUGUENOTS?

Oh, they were the good guys.

-Janet Morgan
(co-pastor Kingdom Ministries International)

Abraham D. Lavender, Ph.D., is a member of the Society for Crypto-Judaic Studies, the Association for the Social Scientific Study of Jewry, and the Huguenot Society of South Carolina. In his book, he states that he believes Huguenots were actually Jews because both Jews and Huguenots believed they were the direct descendants of the twelve tribes of ancient Israel. Because of religious persecution in Spain, Portugal, and France, Jews converted to Christianity yet kept their Jewish traditions in secret. Their cultures and the appearance and customs of both the Huguenots and Jews seemed very similar.

For example:

Protestant Huguenot reformists also called their churches "temples."

The Jewish people and the Huguenots wore similar attire and shared the same first names and surnames.

The Jewish people and the Huguenots lived and worked in the same neighborhoods.

The Sephardic and Huguenot areas of settlement overlapped.

Huguenot reformists were closer to Judaism in practice due to the keeping of the spring and fall feasts of the Lord.

There is a connection between naming patterns and ethnic/religious identity. Huguenot reformists often used Old Testament names for their children, such as Abraham, Isaac, Daniel, David, Jacob, Samuel, and Solomon. Abraham was the only Old Testament name used by Catholics.

Crypto-Judaism is the secret adherence to Judaism while publicly professing to be of another faith. The Huguenots of southern France referred to themselves as living in a desert, which they likened to the Hebrews living in the desert.

The Huguenot shield had a burning bush in the middle with God's name written in Hebrew.

It is interesting to me that the Huguenot refugees fleeing France were some of the finest silk makers in the world at the time. In her book *The Huguenot Church of South Carolina,* Marguerite Couturier Steedman recounts the story of the settling of Charleston by French Huguenots. She speaks of the silkworms aboard the ship *Richmond* "hatching prematurely and dying from want of food."[26] Silk makers, who contributed to France's wealth by virtue of these exports, set up shop in England where they made vast improvements to England's weaving processes negating the need for the coveted silk imports.

The area where my ancestors originated geographically coincides with the location where the Jews fled over the mountains from Spain into Belgium and France. Since borders were guarded to keep Jewish people out during certain periods, many went over the mountains into France. The town of Sedan, home of my ancestors, Suzanne Rochet and Abraham Michaux,[27] is located just 9 miles from the Belgium border. Fabrics used as shrouds and clothing by Bar Kochba rebels who retreated into the cave in the Judahite desert in

---

[26]Steedman, M. (Jan. 1, 1983). *The Huguenot Church of South Carolina.* Nelson Printing Corp. p. 1.

[27]Encyclopedia Britannica. Retrieved from http://www.britannica.com/EBchecked/topic/532102/Sedan

135 C.E., were identified by Israeli archaeologist, Professor Yigael Yadin. Professor Yadin requested the Dexter Chemical Corporation study the colors of the fabrics. "Never before," stated the astonished Dr. Sidney Edelstein, the principal of Dexter and chairman of the Archives Committee of the American Association of Textile Chemists and Colorants, "had such a large varied, old and precisely dated collection of dyed materials been available for analysis."[28]

Dr. Edelstein, together with Dr. David Abrahams, developed a new (positive) technique of separating the elemental dyes from the old fabrics and subjecting the dyes to infrared spectrography. They produced several fascinating conclusions about all the colors used. The intensity of the black colors matched the blacks of the 17th Century Gobelin tapestries of France. They theorized that this was an important clue in the quest to follow the silk weavers of the old Silk Road. These people were known for making a particular kind of dyed silk. I found more evidence when I researched silk making in the hometown of my ancestors at Sedan. "This French town flourished as a cloth-manufacturing center in the 16th and 17th Centuries first under its princes and later under the French King, Louis XIV. Textiles continue to be manufactured in Sedan and the vicinity."[29] Could there be a connection from the clothing found in the Judahite desert in Israel to the Huguenot silk makers in France? Circumstantial evidence implies that it is highly likely.

The fact that Suzanne's parents lamented their daughters having to eat the coarse bread of Holland and the rumors that her mother hid money in her hair with which to buy for them silks and fine dresses for their travel aboard ship to Holland shows that they were financially well-off and could afford to pay the Catholic Church to leave them alone. That the silks were mentioned as being important for the family and that weavers of silk made a lot of money by

---

[28]Kurinski, S. (n.d.). Hebrew History Federation. "Gomez House-The Oldest Jewish Residence in the USA" Fact Paper 30. Retrieved from http://www.hebrewhistory.info/factpapers/fp021_dyemaking.htm.

[29]Encyclopedia Britannica. Retrieved from http://www.britannica.com/EBchecked/topic/532102/Sedan

exporting silks to England and other countries make me think the Rochet family could have been silk merchants or silk weavers as were many Jewish people from certain tribes in ancient Israel. I recall reading something about certain Jews living near the coast of Israel being connected to Huguenot silk makers. These people were known for making a particular kind of dyed silk. Textiles continue to be manufactured in Sedan and the vicinity.[30]

The revocation of the Edict of Nantes of 1685 was followed by a horrendous holocaust, yet it took 15 years for the Manakintowne Huguenots to arrive in Virginia. They came from all over France and escaped to England. The names of the five families who escaped from Sedan were good representatives of the refugees. "One of the five families was named Tipphané (Tiffany) and were from Sedan but emigrated to New York City, where they made their fortunes in jewelry."[31]

The names of the other four families that emigrated to Manakintowne were LeGrand, Rochet, Michaux, and Sublette (Soblet).[32]

After King Charles II of England died in 1685, leaving no heirs, his younger brother succeeded as James II. Roman Catholic King James was on the throne over England, Scotland, Ireland, and Wales, but his constituents were 95% Protestant and had been for over 150 years. His political ambitions were misplaced given the climate, and he mistakenly endeavored to fill high-ranking positions in his military and civil government with Roman Catholics while flagrantly discharging prominent Protestants. Louis XIV had high hopes for

---

[30]Foote, W. H. (1870). *The Huguenots: Or, Reformed French Church. Their Principles Delineated; Their Character Illustrated, Their Sufferings and Success Recorded.* Richmond: Presbyterian Committee of Publication, pp. 242-243. Retrieved from http://www.archive.org/stream/huguenotsorrefor00foot.

[31]Baird, C.W. (1966, 1979). *History of the Huguenot Emigration* 1885.

[32]Brock, R. A. (1962, 1966, 1973, 1979). "Documents Relating to the Huguenot Emigration to Virginia and the Settlement at Manakin-Town 1886." The Vestry Book of King William Parish, Virginia, 1707-1750.

Who Were The Huguenots?

James II of England and felt he would soon convert the populations of England, Scotland, and Wales to Roman Catholicism. The people of England embraced the French refugees and, seeing their condition, became outraged at Louis XIV. King James II reluctantly gave his consent for their care, and a fund was established; communicants of the Church of England, Dissenters called the Huguenots, their brothers, and some Roman Catholics gave liberally to the fund. The battle of the Boyne became known as the League of Augsburg in England. The War of the Grand Alliance banded together nearly "all of the Protestants on the continent and in the British Isles against France and Louis XIV" and "in the British American colonies, the war was known as King William's War."[33]

As the Huguenots were "skilled artisans, master craftsmen, tradesmen" and "artists in all phases of textiles, ceramics, and metals," England found itself unable to "absorb such a sudden influx of such master craftsmen, lace makers, glovers, milliners, jewelers, workers in ceramics."[34] Thus, after fighting so valiantly for King William that led to the signing of the Treaty of Ryswich in the Netherlands in 1697, the Protestant Calvinist king asked how he could best help them. Their leaders decided to brave a voyage to the British American colonies since returning to France and recovering their considerable lands and wealth was not possible.

King William agreed to help the Huguenots get a new start in Virginia; he paid their passages, gave them land, and exempted them from all taxes for seven years. The gift of free passage meant at least a two or three-month voyage across the sea. The four vessels they traveled on were: *Ye Peter, Ye Anthony,* the *Mary Anne,* and the *Nassau.* The King allowed them a liberal diet, and many found themselves better fed on the ships than when they lived in France or England. The group received a land-grant of ten thousand acres on the north shore of the James River. It was for these kindnesses that

---

[33] Sims, W.M. (1993). The Huguenot Society of the Founders of Manakin in the Colony of Virginia. "A Brief History of the Manakin Huguenots." Retrieved from www.huguenot-manakin.org/manakin/Sims.php.

[34] Ibid.

it is said the Manakintowne Huguenots named their assembly "King William Parish." Many made it to Manakintowne and found a good life among the friendly American Indians.

According to Ruth Schecter, an author, and researcher at the Beer Sheva University in Israel, "the Huguenots are identified as the Calvinist Protestants of France though they probably existed before Calvin."[35] Schecter states, "The Calvinists were basically Hebraic in character and mindset, especially when compared to neighboring peoples and religious groups." She writes that the name "Huguenot" was used to refer to these people who only went out at night and practiced their faith near the gate of King Hugo and was used from 1560 on. Hugo is another form of the Hebrew name "Haggi," one of the sons of God (see Genesis 46:16).

Estimates show about 400,000 Huguenots emigrating to Prussia, Holland, Britain, Switzerland, North America, and South Africa after 1685. "The Huguenots displayed strong Israelite characteristics" and came from the French regions in the southeast "where the Goths of Gad had once been present."[36] The Goths believed they descended from Israel. The Jewish people from the French region of Gothia were referred to as Goths. The terms "Jew" and "Goth" "were used synonymously" at the time.

Other historians offer evidence that "the Goths in Southeast France and Spain at some early stage converted to Judaism" and that Jewish Marranos (descended from Sephardic Jews from Spain) became Huguenots. "Jews and Huguenots in France tended to band together," and good evidence shows that during World War II, "the Huguenots of France and the Calvinists of Holland probably more than any other group risked their lives to save Jews from extermination by the Germans."[37]

---

[35] Schecter, R. (n.d.). The Huguenots: Israelite Origins of an Ethnic-Religious Grouping. Adapted with some additions from *The Tribes* Chapter Ten, p. 188. Retrieved from http://www.britam.org/huegenot.html.

[36] Ibid.

[37] Ibid.

Jewish children were placed in Huguenot homes until they could be taken out of France. Hundreds were saved.

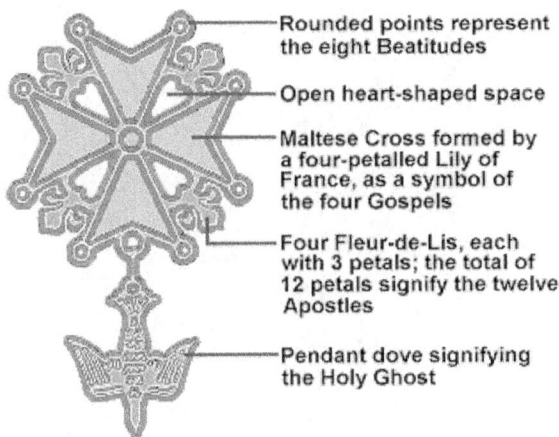

Meaning of the Huguenot Cross

CHAPTER 6

THE REFORMATION

John Calvin and the Huguenots

Since the Huguenots played such a pivotal role in my spiritual DNA, I will address the religion that they embraced; the reformed theology of John Calvin, called Calvinism.

Calvinism is a Protestant theological system and approach to the Christian life. John Calvin was a French theologian important in forming Christian theory during the 1500s. Today, Calvinism refers to the doctrines and practices of the Reformed churches of which Calvin was an early leader.

Calvin's theology was anti-Catholic, influenced by Luther but different in that he sought to cleanse the church of the threads leading back to Constantine. He ended monasteries and celibacy practices for ministers. He simplified worship to include just prayers, singing of psalms, Scripture readings, and a sermon. The church was governed by elected elders. Calvinism denotes people choosing their leaders as in a democracy. John Calvin made a huge contribution to what we know as the Protestant Reformation in the United States[38].

---

[38] Who is John Calvin? What did he do to help the protestant Reformation? Retrieved from https://sites.google.com/site/europeandhowitcamebepowerful/protestant-reformation/who-is-john-calvin-what-did-he-do-to-help-the-protestant-reformati

Though he preached the sovereignty of God to the extent of theorizing about limited atonement, John Calvin was a proponent of the Jewish people and happily affirmed that salvation was of the Jews, that the Christian God originated from the Jews, and that all Christians should embrace the Jewish people, loving them as God loves them because He came first to the Jews. Unfortunately, neither Calvin nor Luther completed the Reformations they began in that they were not able to restore the assembly of believers to its Hebrew roots, the original Primitives. Subsequently, there was no "one new man," Jew and Gentile in Christ, as is happening now in this generation.

My research has shown me that this theologian did not embrace, nor teach replacement theology. It did not originate with him as some have taught. This doctrinal teaching, that the church replaced Israel in the covenant promises and plan of God, arose shortly after Gentile leadership took over from Jewish leadership.

John Calvin did not discount the covenant promises of God to the Jewish people. In all his writings, Calvin was a strong advocate of the Jewish people and defended their rights as the chosen of God. Perhaps this is why the Huguenots embraced Calvinism over the reformed theology of Martin Luther. If they were Crypto Jews, Calvin's worldview would have more closely matched theirs.

Stunning Discovery

The following is from a series of articles by Armand LaFerrere, former adviser to the French minister of the interior, Nicolas Sarkozy, and a member of the board of directors of the Franco-Israeli Friendship Association.

The Jews, The Huguenots and Me - Armand Laferrere[39]

My great-great-great-grandfather was named Moses. My cousins have names like Sarah, Deborah, Jeremy, Judith, Esther, Raphael, and Samuel. My grandfather was hounded by the Gestapo in Paris, and put on a train to Dachau (he survived). My father and uncle have fond memories of their time as kibbutz volunteers in

---
[39]Azure No. 26 - autumn 5767 /2006

the early 1960s. I have had a reasonably good knowledge of the Hebrew Bible since childhood, and during the last Intifada, I took a public stance in France in favor of Israel. Although my language and culture are French, I often feel more comfortable—morally and intellectually—in Israel than I do in my own country.

Yet I do not (as far as I know) have a single drop of Jewish blood in my veins. Neither did I, nor any member of my family, convert to Judaism. But philo-Semitism, which often includes an emotional identification with the Jewish people, is part of the heritage of the community I was raised in: The French Huguenots, or Protestants.

The first thread of a link between our two communities was woven from the very beginning of the history of French Protestantism. What most Jews remember of the European Reformation are, understandably, Martin Luther's anti-Semitic statements. But Luther, with all due respect, is not the father of French Protestantism (there are Lutheran churches in eastern France, but their history is quite different from that of the Huguenots). Rather, our founding father is John Calvin, a Frenchman whose teachings started the most dramatic revolution in Christian-Jewish relations in the history of Christian theology.

The difference between Luther and Calvin on the Jewish question was originally, as always, theological. Luther had broken with the Catholic Church by arguing that salvation is the result not of obedience to any institution, but rather of faith in Jesus Christ. As this condition could obviously not be met by Jews, his initial good will towards them gave way to rage.
There followed a recycling of the worst of the Middle Age blood libels, and hysterical calls for persecution.[40]

In spite of his opposition to the Catholic Church, then, Luther, if anything, only added fodder to the traditional Catholic case against the Jews. Like the Church, he described the Jews as Christ killers and, like the Church, he believed that the Jewish Scriptures contained a "spiritual" meaning that could be understood only by

---

[40]Compare That Jesus Christ Was Born a Jew (1523) to later texts, such as Against the Sabbatarians (1538).

means of the New Testament. Since the Jews followed a "literal" interpretation of these texts and refused to accept their "true" meaning, Luther viewed them as enemies of, rather than precursors to, Christianity.[41] "

Philo-Semitism, which often includes an emotional identification with the Jewish people, is part of the heritage of the community I was raised in: The French Huguenots, or Protestants. But perhaps the most moving example of Protestant efforts on behalf of French Jewry occurred in Le Chambon-sur-Lignon, a small, all-Protestant town in southern France. There, the whole community gave haven to more than three thousand Jews, mostly children, during the war. When a family volunteered to hide a child, Pastor André Trocmé would say, 'I will bring you tomorrow the Old Testament that you have asked for.' Nazi patrols came in search of the Jews repeatedly, but all were safely hidden. Everybody knew, but no one ever spoke.

We are not many. But we French Huguenots-or, at least, those of us who know our own history, are linked with the Jewish people by too many bonds of culture, history, and religious beliefs to betray that old alliance. May the God of Israel give us the strength to proclaim our everlasting gratitude to the Jews. May he give us the grace, which we do not deserve, of sharing their torments today and their victory tomorrow.[42]

It was Armand LaFerrere 's online essay that sent me searching to find out if my own ancestors were of Jewish descent. I discovered that they knew Hebrew. Their ministers taught from the Hebrew bible. They kept the feasts, and gave their children Hebrew names in a culture that did not do that.

---

[41]The accusation of "literalism" is, of course, outrageous when one keeps in mind the extraordinary variety of interpretations of the Jewish Bible in the talmudic and rabbinic traditions. Ignorance of the Talmud, and a systematic refusal to learn about it, may indeed be the largest blind spot in the history of Christian thought

[42]The Huguenots, The Jews, and Me." By Armand Laferrere
Armand Laferrère is a former adviser to the French minister of the interior, Nicolas Sarkozy, and a member of the board of directors of the Franco-Israeli Friendship Association.

Ellis Island and My DNA

As I was poised to type in the name Rochet on ancestry.com, I happened to glance at the sidebar and saw the term: "Jewish genealogy," so I switched sides and found the name Rochet under the subtopic "priority Jewish." Digging deeper, I found a report stating that the families with that surname passing through Ellis Island listed their religious identity as Jewish.

DNA Results:

In 2012, I sent a sample of my blood DNA to be tested by National Geographic after one of my bible study leaders suggested that the reason for my unusual love for Israel, the Jewish people and Hebrew roots of my faith was because of my DNA. At the time, I did not receive it but I never forgot it. *See appendix for test results.

Conclusion

Was it God's hand in my DNA that caused me to recognize Israel as the cornerstone from which my spiritual house was built?

As you continue reading this book, it is my hope that you will see the hand of God connecting the dots from this chapter to the next to see the living waters of God flowing in my journey of faith and discovery, connecting the past with the present.

CHAPTER 7

CONSTANTINE'S SWORD

History of the Huguenots Under Constantine

"Well, would you look at that?" I said to no one in particular while taking a tour of Istanbul, Turkey in 2002. I happened to glance out the window and saw the remnant of an ancient wall sitting on top of a hillside. I was surprised to learn it was part of Constantine's castle.

WOW! What luck to see a thread going all the way back to the time of the Emperor Constantine. I had forgotten that I was in the former city of Constantinople, renamed "Istanbul" by the Turks, when they took the city.

Seeing these ruins was a reminder of Constantine's sword and his influence on the early church. The shadow of his power highlighted and brought into focus the man who is credited with organizing Christianity and turning it into a state religion. However, little is known about who he really was: about the negative, damaging and murderous impact the Christian and Jewish world experienced long after he wielded his sword to sever the church from its roots.

The Original Primitives

Those of the original faith were Jewish. What separated them from their Hebrew (Jewish) counterparts was their belief that their Messiah had come in the person of Jesus. At the time of Jesus' life, there were no Gospels, Epistles, or other books of the New Testament. The persecuted assembly only witnessed the apostles and their followers spread the Good News by word of mouth and covertly copied and circulated through a few letters. Beyond that, the only writings the Jewish people of that day had were tripartite divisions that we refer to as the Old Testament.

The first part, consisting of the first five books of the Bible, was labeled the "Torah," which means "instructions" in Hebrew. The second part was referred to as the book of the "prophets." The third was known merely as the "writings." According to Josephus, all of the Holy Jewish Scriptures are appropriately referred to as the Tanakh and included a total of 22 books. Today, what Christians refer to as the Old Testament consists of 39 books that collectively refer back to the original 22 scrolls except that they were divided up for the convenience of the printers[43].

Lion-headed god standing on a globe with crossed circle.

The Jewish followers of the Messiah, both before and after the crucifixion, were persecuted by non-Messianic Jewish people as blasphemers of the Jewish religion. The division between traditional Jews and Jews who believed that Jesus was the Messiah was clearly defined. Surviving beyond the reach of the Sanhedrin, Jewish believers lived in relative peace up to Constantine's reign (306 to 337 AD). As Constantine reorganized the Christian faith to suit his political ambitions, its Jewish roots were pummeled by edicts that required believers to deny all Jewish roots to the faith, including keeping the Jewish feasts. They had to swear allegiance to the Catholic

---

[43]Associates for Scriptural Knowledge, Restoring the Original Bible, (1976-2014). Chapter 5, *The Proper Numbering of the Books*. Retrieved from http://www.askelm.com/restoring/res005.htm.

Church and end their required Sabbath (Saturday) worship in favor of worship on Sunday in reverence to the sun god. Constantine was interested in ending the Jewish version of Christianity for a pagan version that would embrace him as supreme over the Jewish God and His Messiah.

Constantine made himself vice-regent of Christ on earth and began to persecute Jewish believers and non-believers alike violently. The persecution was subtle at first but later became a matter of survival. Constantine wished to destroy Jewish ties to Christianity along with its promotion of the equality of men under the Lordship of One God for the lordship and resulting oppression of one king (or Emperor)—himself. Just as modern Christians must understand and accept the Jewish roots of their faith, believers must understand and address the changes Constantine wove into the very fabric of our modern faith.

Because we can know by the Scriptures what is important to God, we must seek truth and then live it. When the truth emerges from historical evidence, one can either remove the pagan influences or continue to embrace them. Unfortunately, church leadership and church congregations, faced with the truth, have historically chosen the latter, often denying, compromising, Christianizing, or refusing to accept truth in place of tradition. Christianizing, in this context, means accepting and incorporating pagan influences into Christian religious practices by purposefully changing the original purpose and intent to make it acceptable to Christians, which later became a tradition.

When Martin Luther nailed his 95 Theses to the church door, his complaints primarily revolved around salvation coming by grace alone, and there is one mediator between God and man: Christ, not a priest. This event happened while Roman edicts and pagan influences remained intact.

Constantine's Cultural Influence Today

Constantine claimed to have been divinely called to conquer in the name of Christ and used the cross as his symbol to promote his version of Christianity as the first unified body of believers. He claimed that he saw two swords forming a cross in the rising sun one morning and an inscription that read, "By this cross conquer." What is seldom taught about this period is that Constantine worshiped the ancient Persian god, Mithra, traceable to 6th Century BC and whose symbol was the cross with one line of the cross-connecting the two circles of the zodiac and the other crossing the celestial equator.

As one historian wrote:

Constantine maintained his ties to Mithraism while professing to be a Christian. The rituals of Mithraism were important for the church to carry over to retain favor with the Roman Empire, so it simply adopted them. Customs such as dipping the fingers in holy water and making the sign of the cross were borrowed from Mithraism. The Mithraic cult was male-dominated, with men called "Fathers." The members below them were called "brothers." The Mithraic fathers wore the mitre caps the Christian bishops adopted and still wear today; the Mithraic Holy Father wore a red cap and garment, had an official ring, and carried a shepherd's staff. He was located in Rome. The Christian Bishop of Rome adopted all of these trappings. After the fourth century, the two religions had been blended into the Holy Roman Catholic Church.[44]

The First Council of Nicea

After adopting rituals into the new Christian faith, Constantine used the first Council of Nicea to force other changes to support his purposes. For example, the Jewish calendar based on the lunar cycle was replaced by the Roman solar calendar, and Messiah's accepted death during Passover was replaced by an ancient holiday nearly 3,000 years old at the time. Constantine also declared Rome to be the Holy City in place of Jerusalem and changed the name of Israel to Palestine after Israel's former enemy, the Philistines. The effects of Constantine's rule upon Israel lasted from 306 AD, when he came into power, until 1948 when Israel became an independent state. The fruits of Constantine's agenda survived the Reformation, and

---

[44]Pagan Influence (n.d.). The lion headed god. Retrieved from www.shamarbriyth.com/Paganism/Mithros01.html.

the effects are still seen in churches today. His cobwebs of error were woven into modern doctrine and disrupted the integrity of the original faith that Jesus promoted, and His disciples followed. Although Constantine began persecuting the Jewish people along with Christians who would not embrace his new theology, he also sought to appease the pagans whose support he needed for his political ambitions. He knew it would be difficult to convert them to the new faith unless he included as much of their pagan practices as possible. Thus, he designated their most revered holiday celebrating the birth of the sun god (Tammuz) on December 25th as the date to celebrate Christ's birth. This move caused Christ to be equal in importance to the sun god, and the ritual of celebration became Christ's Mass or Christmas.

He changed the original observance of Jesus' death and resurrection from the Jewish Feast of Passover to incorporate the pagan holiday celebrating the spring fertility rites of the ancient goddess, Ishtar. In doing so, he moved the most sacred of Christian observances away from its Hebraic foundation of Jesus being our Passover Lamb.

Constantine's contemporary, Eusebius of Caesarea, recorded the Emperor's words for those not present at the Council of Nicea, writing just after the Council meeting concluded. The following are quotes from the letter of Emperor Constantine to all who were not present:

> *Relative to the sacred festival of Easter, it was declared to be particularly unworthy for this holiest of all festivals to follow the custom of the Jews. We ought not, therefore, to have anything in common with the Jews. We desire to separate ourselves from the detestable company of the Jews, for it is surely shameful for us to hear the Jews boast that without their direction, we could not keep this feast.*[45]

---

[45]Nicaea Council of 325 A.D. "What Was It All About? - How Did It Change Christianity?" Para. 12. Retrieved from http://www.islamtomorrow.com/bible/NicaeaCouncil325.html.

Thus, the feast celebrating the passion had to take place on a day other than the day that the Jewish people celebrated Passover. Instead, the celebration of the goddess Ishtar (pronounced Easter), also known as Semiramis, became the celebration of the passion or resurrection of Christ. Ishtar can be traced back 25 centuries BC, to the lands of Ur, a Sumerian city-state located in present-day Iraq. In Crete, a similar goddess to Ishtar was worshiped and was later adopted by the Greeks as Aphrodite or Astarte. The Babylonians worshiped Ishtar as Venus referring to her as "The Holy Virgin" and "Queen of Heaven and Earth."[46]

The only change Constantine made was to insert the name of Christ in place of Ishtar which seems innocent enough until one looks deeper. The celebration of Ishtar included sunrise worship on Sunday and the worship of a virgin goddess "variously known as Astarte, Ishtar, Ashtoreth, Cybele, Demeter, Ceres, Aphrodite, Venus, and Freya."[47]

The devastating effect of Constantine's sword has surfaced in many ways throughout the centuries. From the Crusades to the Inquisition, antisemitism was the root cause of Christian religious persecutions, and it continued from 325 AD through to the persecution of the Hussites, the martyrdom of Jan Hus, the persecution and slaughter of the Huguenots, the Pogroms of Europe, and the Holocaust. Thus the Catholic/Protestant conflict began with the original assembly—the Jews who accepted Jesus as Messiah.

After Christianity was severed from its roots, the Church lost its way. Certain passages became obscured and distorted without the benefit of the Jewish culture to make them clear. This left us with erroneous words like predestined, adoption, chosen, and elected by grace that has caused all sorts of problems for the assembly.

---

[46] http://www.cmy.on.ca/newsletters/aug2004.html.

[47] Author unknown (n.d.). "Additional Historical Facts About Easter. Retrieved from http://www.sdadefend.com/Standards/Easter-2.html

CHAPTER 8

TAPESTRY OF SUFFERING

The Crusades

The major watershed of Jewish history in the medieval world is the First Crusade. The Crusades changed all of Jewish life in Europe. It changed the attitude of Christians toward Jews and Jews toward Christians and even Jews toward Jews.

The weeks after Passover are marked as a period of semi-mourning on the Jewish calendar. Among the historical events that happened at this time were the pogroms that accompanied the First Crusade in 1096. Before the Christian Crusaders embarked on their mission to free the Holy Land from the domination of the Moslem infidels, found closer infidels–the Jews–at hand.

It was a dark time in Jewish history and remains as deep and dark a page in the annals of the Christian Church.
For the Jews, the Crusades represented a rude awakening as to their truly precarious position within Christian Europe.

The memory of the Crusades is not only present within us in our commemoration; it exists in the memory of the descendants of the Crusaders.[48]

---

[48]Wein, B. (adapted by Yaakov Astor) (n.d.). "Free Crash Course in Jewish History: The First Crusade." Retrieved from
http://www.jewishhistory.org/the-first-crusade/.

Anti-Semitism:

Threads Woven into the Fabric of the Christian Church:

If you look it up in a dictionary of Church history, you will not find it listed as a systematic study. Rather, Replacement Theology is a doctrinal teaching that originated in the early Church. It became the fertile soil from which Christian antisemitism grew and has infected the Church for nearly 1,900 years. It was introduced to the church shortly after Gentile leadership took over from Jewish leadership. ~ Clarence Wagoner[49]

The five points of replacement theology:
- *Israel (the Jewish people and the land) has been replaced by the Christian Church in the purposes of God, or, more precisely, the Church is the historic continuation of Israel to the exclusion of the former.*
- *The Jewish people are now no longer "chosen people." In fact, they are no different from any other group, such as the English, Spanish, or Africans.*
- *Apart from repentance, the new birth, and incorporation into the Church, the Jewish people have no future, no hope, and no calling in the plan of God. The same is true for every other nation and group.*
- *Since Pentecost of Acts 2, the term "Israel," as found in the Bible, now refers to the Church.*
- *The promises, covenants and blessings ascribed to Israel in the Bible have been taken away from the Jews and given to the Church, which has superseded them. However, the Jews are subject to the curses found in the Bible, as a result of their rejection of Christ.*

Since the Christian Church was born in Acts 2 and the olive tree of Israel, into which we have been grafted, is known to have originated with God's promises to Abraham and his descendants,

---

[49]Wagoner, C.H., (2002). "The Error of Replacement Theology." Retrieved from http://www.therefinersfire.org/replacement_theology.htm.

Christians cannot claim God's promises to the Jewish fathers of the faith and leave out Judah. The olive tree is the nation of Israel. Spiritual Israel consists of those Jews who accept the Messiah (the natural branches) and Gentile believers (wild branches) who are grafted into the same olive tree. Our faith in their Messiah places us among the natural branches, fully accepted and "saved." We have not replaced them. The only reason Christians were given an opportunity to receive salvation was because of the Jewish people's transgression. We await the day when their hearts can receive God's remedy for sin in the person of Jesus.

The Apostle Paul to the Romans:

> *So I now ask, have they (the Jewish people) stumbled so as to fall [to their utter spiritual ruin, irretrievably]? By no means! But through their false step and transgression salvation [has come] to the Gentiles, so as to arouse Israel [to see and feel what they forfeited] and so to make them jealous so that they may return (Romans 11:11 AMP)*

He also affirmed that some of the natural branches were broken off temporarily because of their unbelief.

> *But if some of the branches were broken off, while you, a wild olive shoot, were grafted in among them to share the richness [of the root and sap] of the olive tree, do not boast over the branches and pride yourself at their expense. If you do boast and feel superior, remember it is not you that support the root, but the root [that supports] you. (Romans 11:17-18 AMP)*

By virtue of these passages, serious Christians must remember the gospel was to the Jews first and then to the Gentiles. In Romans 11, Paul states emphatically that the church has not replaced Israel but has joined the olive tree that is Israel. God intends to use us to incite His original chosen ones to jealousy in order to lead them back to Him. So, how can we disregard the very people through whom our Lord came?

Dr. Howard Morgan of HMM (Howard Morgan Ministries) explains:

"As the 'times of the Gentiles' are drawing to a close, God is not only restoring apostolic truth that has been lost to the Church through the centuries, but He is also restoring consciousness to the Church of her Jewish roots. It is extremely important that you understand that the ultimate purpose of this new awareness is the reconciliation between the Church and the Jewish people so that a "jealousy provoking" testimony can come from the Church. Mere academic understanding about the historical roots of the Christian Church or "Jewish" type flavorings for Church services are not the reason for the Holy Spirit's move to restore the Jewish roots of the Christian faith. God's desire is that the Church return to its 1st Century Jewish mindset so that the scriptural purposes for the Church can be accomplished.

The Apostolic truths that are being recovered in many churches, including the great over-arching truth of the unity of the Church, are essential ingredients in the restoration of the Church.

Unless the Church once again becomes the powerful witness that she was at her birth, she will not be able to provoke Israel, or anyone else for that matter, to jealousy.[50]

---

[50]Morgan, H. (n.d.). Retrieved from http://howardmorganministries.org/furthurthoughts.html

Part II

Reflections

Reflections

A little girl, a head full of curls
Became a big sister as I entered the world
When Brenda goofed around, her antics were profound
She often viewed the world on her head upside down
Feet almost touching, heads far apart
Keeping ourselves warm by sharing a cot
Mama tucked us in, pinned the blankets down tight
So we wouldn't crawl out and freeze during the night
Standing on a bench, washing dishes, what a chore
If one stepped off, the other hit the floor
Beans and potatoes, syrup on bread
Were we that poor as some have said?
Eggs from chickens, milk from a cow
If we were not rich, I don't see how
Daddy's woodwork, Mama's sewing
Doll beds and dresses, special love flowing
Learning to skate on a warped wooden floor
Pillows tied to our bottoms, we wouldn't get sore
We had a dog named Panda, special was he
Mama taught him tricks to entertain Brenda and me
Daddy raised tobacco, we labored in the fields
Farm life was work, providing all our meals
From the barn to the stable on an old work horse
I rode home, bareback, of course
Now we are grown with grandkids of our own
Where, oh where, has that time gone?
Memories flood, emotions bind
Two sisters together forever in time.

~Judy Davis

Chapter 9

A Walk Back In Time

The Tobacco Farm

I grew up on a tobacco farm in rural NC and would often roam the woods surrounding my home in search of adventure. I especially enjoyed making playhouses in the woods, pretending to be keeping house. I would string tobacco twine to trees, clear and sweep the ground of debris, set rocks on the ground, put a plank on top, and use them as tables or countertops. Then at other times, I found myself climbing trees to *"skin a cat."* Skinning a cat meant picking out a long tall sapling, bending it over, straddling it, and bouncing up and down just for the fun of it.

My sister and I would turn an empty 55-gallon oil drum onto its side and take turns walking on it while it was rolling in the grass. The object was to see how long we

1952 | Judy (left) and her sister, Brenda, in matching outfits made by their mother

could stay on it before losing our balance and falling off. Once, I tried to build a treehouse all by myself, but my timing could not have been worse because it was in the middle of winter, and I got as far as nailing two boards to a tree before realizing I could not do it alone and relinquished my mission to the cold and went home.

On a different winter day, I tried to show off in front of my cousins by swinging across a nearly frozen creek holding onto a grapevine like Tarzan. But instead of swinging through the air like a bird, I fell into the creek not realizing that in Tarzan's jungle, the birds deposit grape seeds in the *top of the trees* allowing the vines to grow from the top down instead of from the ground up like they did on our land.

1955 | Judy with her doll

I loved to dance so much that I would dance in front of a mirror, pretending I was on stage performing. Later, I took formal tap dance classes and soon began dancing before live audiences in local talent competitions and twice on television.

Summer vacations were like every other month—they offered me no vacation—no break. School's end meant exchanging book work for farm work. My mother worked alongside the men in the fields "priming" or "pulling" the tobacco leaves off the stalks. It was hot, grimy, and physically exhausting work; she was the only woman I knew who would do it. The tobacco tar on the leaves left all our hands blackened and gummy. The workers pulling the tobacco got their clothes sticky with tobacco gum as well, making it necessary to wear long pants, long sleeve shirts, and a hat even in summer to prevent the tar from sticking to their entire body.

Our parents "swapped work" with my uncle and his family during tobacco harvesting time. Before modernization of this process, it required many people working together from dawn to dark to get a barn ready for curing the tobacco leaves. Swapping work helped both households immensely (and simultaneously) by spreading out the workload. Getting the leaves off the stalks to be "housed" in the barn in one day's time was very important.

In spite of the work, growing up on a farm was a wonderful experience. I value it highly and will forever cherish the simple joys of country living. My sister and I were able to spend time building relationships with our cousins and extended family members. Occasionally, I enjoyed riding home from the barn, bareback on our old workhorse. At times like those, I found myself enjoying my simple, uncomplicated life, feeling the setting sun on my back, I was struck with the awesome nature of God's creation and love for his children.

The Lion and the Rock

During the season of my eighth year, I had a vivid dream about the Lord's return. In my dream, I saw and heard a *lion roaring* in the heavens. I ran to my mother and asked her what was happening, and she responded by saying simply, "Jesus is coming."

In my dream, I began jumping up and down when I saw the sky open and Jesus coming in the clouds. I experienced a literal, physical sensation of rising through the air to meet Jesus in the sky. I saw many other people ascending with me, but instead of entering the gates of heaven, I found myself in a field, and the only thing I encountered was a rock. I felt Jesus nearby, but I did not see Him. The dream ended with me turning the rock over and closely examining it. After such a stupendous experience of meeting Jesus in the clouds, the rock was a let-down and was puzzling to my young mind. I did not comprehend it, so I did not mention it to anyone at the time; nevertheless, I woke up, clapping my hands and shouting, "Jesus is coming! Jesus is coming!" Evidently, I was so convincing my father suggested I stay home from school that day. He thought Jesus actually might come.

The dream was so real that it was a long time fading. For about a month, as soon as I got home after school, I would go outside and gaze at the sky, thinking that Jesus might come at that very moment.

At the time, I didn't understand the significance of the lion and the rock, but many years later, after I grew up and viewed it from a biblical perspective, I realized its symbolism. Jesus is the Rock of our salvation, and He is the Lion of the tribe of Judah. I was comforted by this revelation because there were times when I questioned the dream, thinking it might just be the result of my childhood imagination.

The Mountain Top

When I was still eight years old, I had another lucid dream. God took me up on a mountain top near my home and told me to put my ear to the ground. When I did, I heard the Ten Commandments spoken in an audible voice coming out of the mountain. Hearing God speak the Ten Commandments in such a way made me feel like He was embracing me and that I was the focus of His attention. Looking back at that time in my life, I believe these dreams served a purpose. They were spiritual seeds deposited into my innermost being for purposes unknown to me at the time.

During a revival service at a Missionary Baptist Church in 1955, I publicly accepted Jesus as my Savior and followed Him in the believer's baptism. I was 11 years old and still cherish the fact that just like in (the river Jordan) in the days of old, I was baptized in a flowing river. My mother had been raised in a Missionary Baptist Church known today as Southern Baptist but converted to the Primitive Baptist faith after marrying my father, whose family were devout members of that denomination. However, my mother never completely separated from the church of her childhood. She attended special services and sent my sister and me to Sunday school there.

For as long as I can remember, I was exposed to two opposing biblical interpretations of God's plan of salvation. I spent many Sundays listening to Primitive Baptist preachers preaching the "old-time religion" as they called it.

I remember being so hungry to hear the gospel that I liked going to both churches since they both preached the core gospel of salvation by grace through the atoning death and resurrection of Jesus Christ.

Primitive Baptists

Primitive Baptists are a sect that believes theirs is the original or "primitive" form of the gospel, as expressed by Jesus and the disciples. They attempt to stay true to it by clinging to the view that God has chosen a certain number of people out of the world to be saved, and only those chosen and elected to receive His grace will spend eternity with Him in heaven. This is the doctrine of limited atonement. It means that Jesus died only to save those given to Him by His Father God (see Romans 8:30).

Interestingly, Primitive Baptists trace their origin to the New Testament era instead of the reformed teachings of John Calvin, whose writings have been similarly interpreted. They adhere to the same biblical interpretation accredited to Calvin but do not call themselves Calvinists because they reject some of the reformed practices, especially infant baptism.

Missionary Baptists are different from Primitives in that they believe salvation is free for all who believe in and accept the atoning sacrifice of the shed blood of Jesus Christ for their sins (see John 3:16). They send out missionaries because they believe faith comes by hearing the word of God (see Romans 10:17), and everyone has the freedom to receive it. The Primitives, however, do not send out missionaries because they don't believe salvation comes through a person's own free will to receive it.

The difference boils down to the point of when *regeneration occurs.* Does it precede faith? Or, does faith precede regeneration? Does it occur simultaneously? Primitive Baptists believe that regeneration precedes faith and that atonement is limited to only those whom God has chosen out of the world, and their faith is evidence of that regeneration.

With these opposing theologies, I became confused as to the method by which we are saved. I knew I believed in Jesus, but I did not fully comprehend the message of salvation by faith alone in

God's grace because I had been taught by my parents from an early age that saving grace was limited to only those predestined to receive it. Faith itself was a secondary feature of the gospel message.

My mother and other family members would frequently argue about predestination, but neither ever changed their minds. I heard these debates so often that by the time I was grown, those same arguments went round and round in my head, and I could not find any peaceful resolution to them even by reading the Bible. Someone once said that peace comes through understanding. That was certainly true in my case, for I did not understand, and I definitely was not at peace about it. I found that only through the work of the Holy Spirit can one change their biblical world view; debating changes nothing. It took a powerful intervention by God to set me free from such turmoil involving theological debate.

Marriage

I won a college scholarship through the Z. Smith Reynolds Foundation and left home for college in 1963. I was one of 15 girls accepted into the Dental Hygiene program in the School of Dentistry at the University of North Carolina at Chapel Hill. At that time, UNC-CH and Florida State were the only schools on the East Coast offering a Dental Hygiene curriculum. After passing the State Board Exams, I began work at a private dental practice in Winston-Salem, North Carolina. One day a new patient showed up in my dental chair wearing a baseball cap and a wide grin. He loved farming, and I was a farmer's daughter. Soon, he asked me out and captured my heart. Jesse Shumate Davis, Jr. and I were married in 1967. The first of our two sons was born three years later.

Now married and in my mid-twenties, my life seemed complete. However, I felt a void in my heart and soul regarding my spiritual condition. My spiritual house was divided. Though I *"walked the aisle"* to receive Jesus as my Savior at age eleven, there was still a battle going on inside me that needed to be resolved. One side said I did not need to accept Christ because it was already a done deal, and the other side said if I did not accept Christ, I would be condemned to hell.

There were so many things in God's word that I did not understand, so I began searching for a deeper intimacy with God by reading books. I even wrote to Billy Graham.

The Doctrine of Limited Atonement

The doctrine of limited atonement prevented me from having the kind of relationship with Jesus that I so desperately wanted and needed. How could a God of love and a God who predestined souls to hell be one and the same? Fortunately, God led me to the altar of my husband's Moravian church in 1971. It was in that lovely congregation of Moravians that God answered my heart cry and brought me out of my despair. He healed the breach created in my childhood.

The Moravians

The Moravian Church has a long and colorful history beginning in 1457, but its roots go back to the reforming efforts of Jan Hus (1369-1415, often referred to in English as John Hus or John Huss). The Moravians are the oldest known Protestant Church and the earliest recorded Christian sect to protest Catholicism. They did not originate from the rule of Constantine, as did other reformists. The Hussites (or Moravians) had a desire to remain true to pre-Constantine Christianity, which means a return to the teaching of the New Testament alone.

Moravians originated in the 9th Century when two Greek Orthodox missionaries, Cyril and Methodius, reportedly brought Christianity to Bohemia and Moravia, known today as the Czech Republic.[51] Under them, the countries established a national church and translated the Bible into their common language. Originally known as the Unity of the Brethren, they were an illegal church separate from the Roman Catholic Church and often suffered intense persecution.

---

[51]*Moravian Church in North America* (2000-2012). Retrieved from http://www.moravian.org/the-moravian-church/history/

The next 400 years saw Bohemia and Moravia come under Roman religious jurisdiction, causing an uprising of protesters who wanted to keep to the original faith. These protesters were reportedly led by Jan Hus, a professor of philosophy and rector of the University in Prague. Hus was the primary founder of the modern-day Moravian Church. These protesters, originally called Hussites, met at the Bethlehem Chapel in Prague, where Hus preached and formed a Protestant bloc against many Roman Catholic practices. In the end, Hus paid for his beliefs with his life and was used as an example to protesters of Constantine's new organized faith. Hus endured a lengthy heresy trial and on July 6, 1415, was tied to a stake and burned alive as the priest read a declaration:

> *O cursed Judas because you have abandoned the councils of peace, and have counseled with the Jews, we take from you the cup of redemption.*[52]

Hus died because he supported the Christian conviction that believers should be able to hear and read the Scriptures in their own language (see Acts 2:6). It was this same conviction that inspired John Wycliffe to translate all 80 books of the Bible into English, which he completed in 1382, two years before his death. It is reported that Wycliffe translated 80 books, including the Apocrypha between the Old and New Testaments, instead of the 66 we have today claiming it was for historical purposes. These 80 books remained in the King James Version for 275 years but were not regarded as equal to the holy and inspired word, so were removed in 1885.[53]

Hus supported Wycliffe's notions and made translations of all 80 books for his followers to read as well. Wycliffe also referred to gathering places as "assemblies" rather than churches because the Greek word for "church" referred to pagan gatherings, whereas the

---

[52]Carroll, J. (2001). *Constantine's Sword: The Church and the Jews, A History.* New York: Houghton Mifflin Company, p. 338.

[53]Jeffcoat III, J.L. (2011). Retrieved from: http://www.greatsite.com/timeline-english-bible-history/#timeline.

original Greek word for "assemblies" referred to Jewish gatherings. It is fascinating that today, the word "church" trumped "assemblies" as the official name for the gathering of believers. During the time of Jan Hus, the Catholic Church was struggling to maintain order and a consistent flow of money through taxes and pardons. It needed to keep resistances and uprisings under control.

To explain the struggles endured by Bohemian Christians at the hands of the church, Hus wrote,

> *One pays for confession, for mass, for the sacrament, for indulgences, for churching a woman, for a blessing, for burials, for funeral services and prayers. The very last penny which an old woman has hidden in her bundle for fear of thieves or robbery will not be saved. The villainous priest will grab it.*[54]

The Hussites pressed on after Hus was lost to them and gradually were known as Moravians because of Moravia, the territory from which they came. In 1457, they restructured their church in the village of Kunvald, Bohemia, just 60 years before Martin Luther's Reformation and 100 years before the Anglican Church was established. In Bohemia, Protestantism reached 90% popularity in the decades that followed Hus' death. The Moravian Church thus established its strength, and by 1517 they were about 200,000 strong with over 400 recognized communities and two printing presses.[55]

The Moravians and Count Zinzendorf

Despite their numbers, the Moravians were persecuted and driven into Poland and other areas. Count Nicholas Ludwig von Zinzendorf, a Saxony nobleman, and Moravian sympathizer offered up his estate to fleeing Moravians in 1722 and built a haven for refugees in the community of Herrnhut. The Moravians were literally saved from extermination through the generosity of the Count, who provided

---

[54]Macek, J. (1958) *The Hussite Movement in Bohemia*, Orbis, Prague, p. 16.

[55]Moravian Church in North America (2000-2012). Retrieved from http://www.moravian.org/the-moravian-church/the-moravian-church/history.html.

the means for the persecuted Moravians to migrate to the West Indies and subsequently to North America. Count Zinzendorf sent the first Moravian missionaries to the West Indies in 1732, where they rescued many oppressed Negro slaves suffering in St. Thomas and other islands. The Moravians saw extreme manipulation and violence perpetrated against the slaves and reported that the atrocities were so cruel as to be beyond description.

> *Count Zinzendorf had a heart for Israel and loved the Jewish people. It has been said that it was Zinzendorf's blessing upon the Jewish people that provided the legal ground for God's blessing to come upon the Moravians.*
> *And I will bless those who bless you [who confer prosperity or happiness upon you] and curse him who curses or uses insolent language toward you; in you will all the families and kindred of the earth be blessed [and by you they will bless themselves](Genesis 12:3 AMP)*

God's favor followed the Moravians as they migrated out from the Count's protective lands and to the West Indies and then to the United States in 1735. They tried to settle in Savannah, Georgia, under the direction of General Oglethorpe, but the colony eventually failed.[56]

Interestingly, John Wesley and his brother Charles encountered the Moravians when they were on a ship bound for Savannah during this period. During their four-month journey, a terrible storm arose and broke the main mast of their ship. John Wesley reported that while the Englishmen on board were crying for their lives, he was amazed to find a group of Moravians calmly singing hymns and praying. He was deeply moved by their stoic composure and faith, and it was this experience that changed the course of his preaching for the rest of his life.

Once they safely landed on the Georgian coast, Wesley, as the appointed missionary in Savannah, ministered from 5:00 in the morning to 4:00 in the afternoon and then joined the Moravians as

---

[56]Ross, K.W. and Stacy, R. (June, 2013). *John Wesley and Savannah* Retrieved from http://www.sip.armstrong.edu/Methodism/wesley.html.

their student. Two years later, John Wesley returned to England on the 22nd of December, 1737.

Upon his return to London, John Wesley, still enamored with their strong faith, continued to worship with the Moravians on a regular basis. Meanwhile, the American Moravians continued their migration into colonial America, arriving in Pennsylvania in 1741.[57] There they created a permanent presence, first colonizing on the estate of George Whitefield, who was a friend and contemporary of Wesley. Soon, Moravians began to purchase thousands of acres of land in the regions of Bethlehem and Nazareth, there establishing a strong agricultural and industrial presence there. These establishments flourished both in the north and south with a large influx of Moravian immigrants from Europe who finally felt safe enough to follow their contemporaries into the new regions.

The Moravian sect has endured a long and tumultuous past but survives today, a fragmented bloc of sincere Christians who have parishes in 16 states as well as a presence in the southern island regions and in South Africa.

The Intervention

Its Glowing

Knowing this brief history of the Moravians makes my salvation experience at my husband's church much more dear to me. It was there where I first received confirmation and the assurance that I could actually know I was saved. I remember the day vividly. It was as if the altar of this Moravian assembly actually called me forward; my heart inside me was yearning for God. The moment I stepped out into the aisle, I began to feel a tingling sensation in my body. By the time I reached the altar, a brilliant white light suddenly exploded inside me. At that moment, I saw and experienced the Lord Jesus Christ but not as a visual image. I was feeling His essence, followed by an awakening that reached into the very core of my being.

---

[57]Moravian Church in North America (2000-2012). Retrieved from: http://www.moravian.org/the-moravian-church/the-moravian-church/history.html.

As I stood at the altar, the Pastor smiled at me kindly and took hold of my hands. At that moment, the truth of the gospel became a living reality. I was flooded with an awesome, powerful force.

What I had known before as only a theological concept, slipped into my soul as the truth. Suddenly, I felt the physical sensation of shackles being broken off and ripping away from the boundaries of my heart.

Still fully immersed in the encounter, I saw the light shining forth from the Pastor's eyes. I did not comprehend at the moment that this light was a reflection of the illumination emanating from me. The Shekinah glory of God had descended, and it affected the pastor as acutely as it had affected me, for he gasped audibly and took a step back, *staring at me*. When I turned away to return to my seat, I heard him say, "Look at her face. It's glowing!"

I had accepted Jesus as the Messiah in my youth but had no assurance of my salvation. The Primitive Baptists do not believe one can know they are saved.

They believe theirs is a "hope so" religion, verbalized as such by many of its members. Up until that moment, I kept telling myself that since I did not drink, smoke, or knowingly disobey God's commandments, I must be okay and would go to heaven when I died.

Not understanding the sinful condition the descendants of Adam and Eve are born into, I fell into the trap that the majority of humanity falls into—that being good according to the law of our own conscience is good enough to get us into heaven after we die. But at that glorious altar, I discovered the awesome shame of standing before a pure and Holy God, clothed only in the filthy rags of my own self-righteousness. Then, in a moment, in the *twinkling of an eye*, I was at His mercy seat, totally cleansed by the blood of the resurrected Savior. Hallelujah!

Author Ray Comfort explains it like this:

> *A little girl remarked to her mother how clean some sheep looked against the green grass. Then as snow began to fall this same girl noticed how dirty the sheep looked against the white snow. The*

background made all the difference. If you and I judge ourselves using the background of human standards, we come up quite clean. We can find plenty of people who are worse than us. Until the snow fell, the girl did not know what real purity was.[58]

Songs like "The Old Rugged Cross" and many other hymns from my childhood, leaped off the pages of time and became a living, breathing reality inside me. The Pastor of this Moravian church said he had never seen anything quite like what happened to me. It jolted him into a new reality: that of reconsidering tradition. Subsequently, he began conducting home Bible studies to examine this new wave of the Holy Spirit's baptism of fire. All his life, he said he had ministered according to tradition, believing the fire that birthed the church at Pentecost (Shavuot) was a one-time occurrence. But after what happened to me, he wanted to know if that same fire was available to us, as so many believers were claiming during the early 1970s.

God's Heart — God's Fire

The same year that Israel became a nation in 1948, fresh Holy Ghost fire, complete with speaking in tongues, fell on a group of Catholic Nuns at Notre Dame University, which quickly spread into what is now known as the Charismatic Renewal.

My dear Pastor Helmich took me to a few Full Gospel Fellowship Meetings. I was at one of those meetings when he said to me, "I've seen a Catholic priest and a Protestant minister putting their arms around each other confessing their love for Jesus."

Years later, in Israel, I heard the testimony of a Messianic Jewish pastor at Mt. Carmel Assembly in Israel say, "I have seen it over and over. When a Palestinian and a Jew are born again in the Messiah, the walls come down between them. They love each other in the Messiah. No longer is there an issue." Praise God! It wasn't long before the hidden threads in my DNA began to draw me even closer to where His divine will was taking me.

---

[58]Comfort, R. (1989). *Hell's Best Kept Secret*. Whitaker House. p. 133.

Living Waters

CHAPTER 10

LIVING WATERS

He that believes in me, as the scripture has said, out of his belly shall flow rivers of living water.

John 7:37 - NKJV

Angel in My Closet

My husband and I shared a house with his widowed father, whom I affectionately referred to as Mr. Davis. We lived there from 1967 until a few years after his death in 1975. In addition, several other members of his family lived in the same house with us at various times during that period.

The rooms and main living area were small and open with little privacy. Because of this, I began using one of the tiny bathrooms as my place to pray. Just behind the bathroom door was a small linen closet. Once inside the room, I had to back up against the sink, turn and face the linen closet before I could close the bathroom door. After that, there was just enough room to kneel at the toilet to pray. Although cramped, this little bathroom became my sanctuary.

Because my husband worked the second shift, I was alone with his father and my firstborn son at night. I often went to prayer meetings or Bible studies in the evenings. Mr. Davis enjoyed taking care of his grandson, but he was not always supportive of my extracurricular church activities. He was very quiet about his faith, and although I saw him reading his Bible every night, the few times that the supernatural came up, he expressed skepticism. In contrast, I was quite vocal about my ongoing understanding and revelations about God.

Mr. Davis was there the day of my life-changing experience at the altar of the Moravian church, but he never mentioned it. One night, while I was preparing to go to the parsonage for a women's Bible study, his demeanor clearly indicated that he did not want me to attend. By the time I went to draw my bath to get ready, I was so distraught and feeling upset that I was going against his wishes that I began thinking I should stay home. Once in the bathroom, I performed my ritual to get the bathroom door closed, and upon facing the linen closet, I came face to face with the supernatural. An angel was in my bathroom!

I was so startled and shocked, I simply froze. Its perimeter (outer form defining its shape) glowed while the rest was semi-transparent. It began fading away the moment I came in contact with it; however, what the angel left behind flooded into my spirit and soul. I was pierced with the most exquisite feeling of God's love and comfort. Supernatural warmth permeated every cell of my body. It was tangible, and beyond anything I can describe. The Holy Spirit filled every corner of that tiny bathroom along with my entire being. I remember thinking, "If this is what heaven is like, I want to go right now."

Had it not been for the incredible effect the angelic presence deposited in that room and inside me, I might have doubted what I saw. Was it a ministering angel or a guardian angel sent to comfort, strengthen, and encourage me, or to prepare me for some future event? Did it have more than one purpose? I can only speculate, but that night I went to my prayer meeting as scheduled and stunned everyone when I told them about what had just happened to me.

For about a month every morning thereafter, Mr. Davis found me sitting in the quietness of his living room, reading my Bible, and trying to hold on to that precious encounter through the written Word. Then one morning, his curiosity got the better of him, and he asked me why I was getting up so early and reading my Bible. He knew I was a night owl with no inclination to get up at the crack of dawn, so I told him about what had happened in the bathroom and the effect it had had on me. I was both surprised and glad to hear him say, "Well, I guess you had a vision."

He never mentioned it again, but he began spending quality time with me discussing the Bible and spiritual things. He became much more open about his faith. I believe the angel in my bathroom opened a window that allowed a more trusting, spiritual relationship between us.

A few weeks before he passed away, he began watching a local evangelical preacher on television while I was at church. For several weeks, he would speak about what he had heard on the telecast and would say to me, "You know, I believe it. I believe it." I took those statements as an affirmation and verbal confession of his faith.

> *The supernatural world cannot be explained through science or the laws of nature; it can only be seen through faith. The metaphysical world is abstract and without form. It is beyond what we can see and includes the philosophical study of the nature of being and how we relate to the supernatural world. Although the metaphysical world is without form, most human beings embrace our unseen world as a fascinating part of it.*

Despite the lack of privacy in my father-in-law's home, I believe my time spent sharing spiritual matters with him helped build his faith and gave him the ability to express it. The bridge that was built between Mr. Davis and me was important to both of us and to the family he left behind.

Chapter 11

Quenching the Spirit

The Veil Thins

In May of 1972, I got an early morning phone call with the devastating news that my beloved Moravian Pastor had died suddenly of a heart attack. I remember sitting in the parsonage just a few hours later when I distinctly heard him speak my name, so close to my ear, I could almost feel his breath on it. Pastor Helmich had a unique accent, and there was no mistaking it. I was so startled that I literally jumped in my seat and looked around the room for him. My automatic response came into play in spite of knowing full well he had departed this world. A dear friend in his congregation later told me the same thing had happened to her—he called her name as she was walking to her car on the way to work.

I believe the veil becomes thin between this world and the next when someone close to us dies. I never doubted that it was my Pastor. That sweet man was just saying goodbye, and because of my physical reaction, I believe he knew I had heard him.

Quenching the Fire of the Holy Spirit

After Pastor Helmich died, I was asked to teach the senior high/post-high Sunday school class, and I accepted but quickly found myself going through a fire of a different kind.

Our church went through a difficult period while the elders searched for his successor. It was nearly a year before they replaced him with a handsome young man fresh out of the Moravian Seminary. He arrived when the fire of the Holy Spirit was spreading fast among the churches.

Even in formerly resistant congregations, many parishioners had become open to this new move of God. Unfortunately, our new Pastor planned to quench this spiritual shift. I was very vocal about my faith and frustrated at the lack of connection between us. Once, while sitting in the living room of my home, he spoke about how he admired my faith while at the same time lamenting the fact that his faith had been destroyed in seminary.

Later, he told me in a private conversation that he, along with a few others in his counsel, had decided to frown upon all references to the Holy Spirit in any songs sung during services and that he planned to eliminate them. He specifically mentioned the song, "Sweet Holy Spirit—You are welcome in this place."

I walked out of his office that day, totally stunned. I was literally shaking in disbelief. In the end, he effectively put out the spiritual passion that was taking root in our congregation. Even so, it continued to burn hot within me as I struggled to hold on to the gifting and power that the Holy Spirit had so freely given.

Teaching my Sunday school class and sitting under this young pastor's leadership was difficult and discouraging. One day, he sat in on my class when I was teaching about the Second Coming of Christ. The David C. Cook Sunday School Quarterly lesson that day taught that one of the signs of His return would be that the Jewish people would be back in their promised land. When I finished, I asked him for his thoughts, to which he said, "That land over there has been changing hands for thousands of years. I don't believe we are any closer to Jesus coming back than we were two thousand years ago." I wondered if he thought Jesus was never coming back.

Discernment

It wasn't long before I was asked to review new material under consideration in place of our traditional Sunday School Quarterly.

I was shocked and dismayed to find myself reading a very liberal, faithless interpretation of Scripture. It set forth a religious view that dismantled the biblical foundation of God's Word and ripped the very heart out of the first five books of the Bible (the Torah). It treated all supernatural phenomena as symbolic rather than literal. This created a real crisis for me because I knew I could not teach it in good conscience. The end result was it caused me to lose faith in the corporate church hierarchy that was now accepting and pushing faithless theology.

The program was known as the Covenant Life Curriculum. Introduced in the early 1960s, it became a point of division within the Southern Presbyterian Church and, arguably, may have been a final factor in the 30-year struggle between the conservative Southern Presbyterians and the extremely liberal Northern Presbyterians. This struggle concluded with conservatives breaking away from the Northern Presbyterian Church and also led to the formation of the "PCUSA" (Presbyterian Church in the United States of America) in 1973.[59]

Covenant Life Curriculum was criticized by conservative Presbyterians because they believed it was heavily influenced by the neo-orthodoxy of Karl Barth and Emil Brunner. Barth took a neo-orthodoxy (traditional) approach to Christianity when mere moralism and humanism had seemingly won over the theological world. Conservatives, on the other hand, wondered about Barth's orthodox version of theology because he refused to consider the Bible to be "infallible."

Karl Barth not only said, "The gospel is not a truth, among other truths. Rather, it sets a question mark against all truths," but he spent his life posing question marks in the name of Christ against all manner of "truths." In the process, he did nothing less than alter the course of modern theology, i.e., the study of the nature of God and religious belief.

---

[59]PCA Historical Center (n.d.). "The Covenant Life Curriculum." Retrieved from http://www.pcahistory.org/findingaids/pcus/covenantlife.html.

In Berlin, he sat under the teachings of famous liberals of the day like historian Adolf Harnack who taught an optimistic view of Christianity that focused not so much on the fatherhood of God or the cross but on Jesus Christ as the brotherhood of man.[60]

Emil Brunner, a contemporary of Barth, proposed that God revealed Himself not just in the Bible but in nature as well (though not in a saving way). These two men agreed on their theology but disagreed strongly on the idea of natural theology. Brunner affirmed that God could be known, and grace could be found by means other than through biblical revelations of Jesus Christ. For example, He can be known by revelations gleaned through the study of God's creations rather than revelations about Christ, alone. In contrast, Barth believed God is unknowable except through revelation. Even so, Barth's work did not support traditional Christianity but instead favored non-fundamentalist ideas such as neo-orthodoxy's critical evaluation of social institutions leading to liberation theology. According to an online encyclopedia, liberal theology is "an umbrella term covering diverse, philosophical, and non-mystic biblical text beliefs within general Christianity that became more popular in the 20th Century."[61]

For a time, Covenant Life Curriculum became the authorized curriculum of five denominations: the Associate Reformed Presbyterian Church, the Cumberland Presbyterian Church, the Moravian Church in America, the Presbyterian Church in the United States, and the Reformed Church in America.[62]

This curriculum taught many errors, including one that asserted that the twelve tribes of Israel originated randomly. I knew the Bible taught that God blessed Abraham and made a lasting covenant with

---

[60]Gali, M. (Jan 1, 2000). Christianity Today, "Christian History—Neo-Orthodoxy: Karl Barth." Issue 65. Retrieved from http://www.christianitytoday.com/ch/2000/issue65/5.23.html.

[61]Wikipedia. Retrieved from http://en.wikipedia.org/wiki/Liberation_theology.

[62]PCA Historical Center. The Covenant Life Curriculum of the Presbyterian Church in the United States (PCUS). Retrieved from http://www.pcahistory.org/findingaids/pcus/covenantlife.html.

him and his descendants beginning with his son, Isaac, and Isaac's son, Jacob. The Bible said God's blessings over Abraham continued to the house of Jacob, who had twelve sons, and these sons became the leaders of the twelve tribes of Israel; they were not representative of a random number. The curriculum I reviewed consisted of several books. In one of these books, parts of the Bible, such as Proverbs, were compared to Aesop's fables. After reading all this, I knew I had a choice to make regarding this new theology.

Painful though it was, I concluded that no matter what the repercussions would be, I could not teach it. Shortly afterward, I resigned from my teaching post but remained in the Moravian church for several more years. As a result of my resistance as the teacher and leader of a senior high/post high class, this apostate view of the Bible failed at my church. The curriculum did not survive in the southern province of the Moravian church either.

Saying Goodbye

Leaving this sweet congregation, my friends and my Sunday School class was a self-inflicted exile that sent me into the wilderness; although, I still loved my Savior. It took many years, and my father's death before I found my way back into another fellowship.

As the Spirit began to stir me to get back into an assembly of believers, I briefly united with another Moravian church. I recall sitting there in one of the most liberal churches in its southern province, arguing with God about how it was okay to attend services in this Moravian church because the Pastor seemed to love the Lord. Did it matter if he didn't believe in Old Testament miracles, biblical prophecy, or the first five books of the Bible? I later saw that I was so spiritually asleep that setting foot in a church again seemed to be enough for me. What I did not realize was that God was going to use my experience there to wake me up.

As I became spiritually aware and hungry for what I once had, the dry bones of this assembly caused me to thirst again for His well of living water. Thus, I ended my association with the denomination that had once been such a blessing to me, and I began to look elsewhere to find His absolute will and purpose for my life.

Part III

Grabbing That Sword Again

CHAPTER 12

THE JOY OF THE LORD IS MY STRENGTH

Finding the Well

My opportunity to find fellowship again came one day in 1996 when I attended a watercolor painting class. During lunch, Margaret Wilson, a fellow artist, spoke about her Sunday evening prayer and praise services at Reynolda Presbyterian Church. As soon as the words came forth from her mouth, my spiritual antennae shot up, and I knew I had to visit. I had drunk from that well of living water once before, and after nearly 20 years in the desert, I was ready to pick up the sword of the Spirit again. I exclaimed, saying, "I want to go," and go, I did!

The local assembly she referred to was an Evangelical Presbyterian Church in Winston-Salem, which was formed in 1961 after it split from the Bible Presbyterian Church in 1956. It separated from the PCUSA to embrace the Charismatic Renewal. And praise the Lord. Members were free to practice the five-fold ministry (see Ephesians 4:11-13).

Margaret was startled at my response because she had never known me to be a churchgoer, let alone a Charismatic! Of course, she couldn't have known that I had taught Sunday school years earlier or that I had been baptized in the Holy Spirit's fire as I had never spoken of these things. Even though I had never lost my love for

God or my faith in Jesus' work on the cross, I had no witness or Christian testimony in my life that anyone could discern. Something within me instinctively knew that the Sunday evening services at this church were going to be like those I had attended at Full Gospel Business Men's meetings so many years before. After years of being out of fellowship and worshiping alone, perhaps even cynical in my frustration with the church, the Lord was miraculously leading me back into His arms. Soon my faith in Christian fellowship was restored, and my spirit soared.

Weeping for Joy

After my first visit, I was hooked. For weeks after the evening services, I went home weeping with joy. I had literally found the water for which my soul had been craving. It was at Reynolda that I discovered my Jewish roots and began to embrace what I felt was missing in my spiritual life.

Instinctively, I knew that God was going to launch me back into ministry. At the time, I had no idea what He had in mind. I was just rejoicing to be back in a Spirit-filled assembly! Soon I took a class called "Experiencing God" by Henry Blackaby, and God used this experience along with the facilitator and students to begin to heal and bind up the wounds of my past.

Susan Miller

When I first came to Reynolda, I met a dynamic woman of God who patted the empty pew seat beside her and invited me to sit down. I was so blessed by her upright character and love for God that I asked Him to put her in my path again. *He soon did.*

I shared a house with her during my first Women of the Word conferences at Christian Believers United (CBU). I joined Susan's Bible study class, where she was teaching on the Tabernacle, and before I knew it, we were traveling together on my first mission trip to Jamaica.

Susan and I went to Israel together as volunteers with Barry and Batya Segal's Vision for Israel and The Joseph Storehouse Humanitarian Aid Center in 2001. During one of her Bible studies, we focused on the book, *Our Father Abraham,* by Marvin Wilson of Gordon-Conwell University. His teaching, along with many other Hebraic teachings, positioned me to learn more about our Hebrew God and that precious tree in which we Christians are grafted into. I couldn't seem to get enough of this living water. I read *Israel, My Beloved* by Kay Arthur, and later, Susan, Debbie Hill, and I, along with a few others, formed a group called *"For Zion's Sake."*

Based on Isaiah 62 and born out of our understanding of God's love for and promises to Israel, we focused not only on prayer support for Israel but also on education and support for others interested in God's covenant promises to the Jews as well as all believers. For Zion's Sake stoked the fires that had begun to burn in the hearts of many in Reynolda's congregation to express love for Israel and the Jewish people.

Vision for Israel - The Joseph Storehouse

In the late 1990s, I traveled with a few of my Bible study friends to participate in CBU's first Judeo-Christian Conference in Montreat, North Carolina. This became an annual event. After studying the book, *Our Father Abraham,* by Dr. Marvin Wilson, it was a special treat to hear the author speak at the conference. At the same event, I had the pleasure of meeting the conference worship leaders, Barry and Batya Segal.

Though primarily a musician and singer, Barry also led one of our breakout seminars. This Messianic husband and wife team later formed an international ministry that included The Joseph Storehouse. Through their ministry, Vision for Israel, they collect donations and supplies from all over the world for distribution to those in need residing in Israel, including the Arab population. In addition to the Storehouse, they currently produce the JNN News Report plus Roots and Reflections, a television show about the land, the people, and the culture of Israel. Currently, they are expanding the Vision for Israel/Joseph Storehouse Outreach Ministry by constructing the new Millennium Center in Israel."[63] The Segals played an important role in the next phase of my life. Batya is a gifted songwriter and singer. She and Barry record and produce worship CDs with a Hebraic flavor. The moment they began to lead us in worship, I began to weep. I tried to manage my emotions, but I couldn't get a grip on myself. I found myself weeping to the point of wailing. The Hebrew music began to seize my heart and take me to a spiritual place both foreign and familiar.

I didn't understand it at the time, but God was using the music to draw me toward a new life path. Their Jewish-flavored music was uncovering a hidden thread in my spirit that would change the course of my life in ministry work. It was at this conference that I first began to understand and connect some aspects of my genealogical past to my present heritage.

Years later, at a VFI Joseph's Storehouse Conference, in Savannah, Ga, I experienced a deep emotional impact when I heard the keynote speaker, Dr. Jim Goll, deliver a message about the Moravian leadership in Herrnhut, Germany. In addition to relating the history of Count Zinzendorf to our group that night, Jim also testified about a recent dispute involving the leaders of various Moravian congregations in Herrnhut who had come together to debate the issue of the Baptism in the Holy Spirit, (the same supernatural occurrence some had experienced at my Moravian church in 1973). He shared that during the debates, God supernaturally knocked those quarreling leaders off their feet, and all of them experienced the fire of His Spirit.

Sadly, the historical Moravian church that had once believed in God's supernatural acts were now represented by leaders who were meeting to dispute them. But, in that one small town of historical significance, a handful of Moravians came to know God's Spirit and once again experienced the Unitas Fratrum, the Unity of the Brethren.

---

[63] To learn more about Vision for Israel and The Joseph Storehouse, visit http://www.visionforisrael.com or see their guest appearance on The 700 Club http://www.cbn.com/700club/guests/bios/Barry-Segal-101410.aspx.

Unitas Fratrum in the Worldwide Moravian Church consists of Unity Provinces, Mission Provinces, Mission Areas, and specific areas of work that are the responsibility of the Moravian Unity as a whole. They are termed Unity Undertakings.[64]

By the time the Hussite Assembly was given refuge on Count Zinzendorf's estate, they were a quarreling splintered congregation until an outpouring of God's Holy Spirit fell on them, bringing them into unity and peace. They held a feast of love from which the present-day Unity of the Brethren (Moravian) Lovefeast originated.

That night, God revealed why it was such an affront to me when I was asked to teach the new material from Covenant Life Curriculum. He pulled back the curtain of time and began showing me what my spirit already knew; His hand in the hidden threads of my DNA caused me to recognize the movement for what it was—subversion. At that conference, I realized Israel had been the cornerstone upon which rested the reconstruction of my spiritual life. I believe that because I refused to teach the liberalized, false doctrine in my Moravian Sunday school class, God provided the foundation for me some twenty years later to move forward in a new ministry according to His perfect timing.

Standing in the Gap

During the VFI conference, Dr. Goll introduced the concept *of identification repentance.* He explained that God was calling His people to stand in the gap and repent for the sins committed by the early church in the name of Christianity. He explained how we could identify the sins, stand in the gap for them, and repent for them. He shared a revelation and prophetic biblical principle and teaching from the Lord that identification repentance had to happen before Jesus would come to cleanse His temple (the assembly) of all the crimes done in His name.

---

[64] Unitas Fratrum: The Moravian Unity of the World Wide Moravian Church. Retrieved from http://www.unitasfratrum.org

That night, Gentile Christians began to weep and wail in response to his strong message. Some came forward, knelt in front of Barry and Batya Segal *(whose DNA represented their Jewish ancestors)*. They asked for forgiveness for what the church had done to the Jews in the name of Christianity.

Years later, God brought to my attention the existence of another group persecuted by the church in a bloody witch-hunt that scattered them throughout Europe and across the Atlantic to America. These were my ancestors—the French Huguenots.

2008 | Hebraic Art In Worship

We will [shout in] triumph at your salvation and victory, and in the name of our God we will set up our banners. May the Lord fulfill all your petitions (Psalm 20:5 AMP).

CHAPTER 13

HIS BANNER OVER ME IS LOVE

My mother had no idea of the implications when she named me *Judy Gail*. In Ivrit Hebrew, my name is *Y'hudit Gayil* גיל יהודית meaning one who casts the hand in praise to Yah rejoicing. *Yah hoo deet (feminine for the root word, Judah or Y'hudah)* and *guy yil or Judy Gail,* means one who praises the Lord in dance and banners and raises her arms to God in worship. *"The name Judah appears to be associated with the verb* ידה *(yada), meaning to praise."* [65] In Genesis we learn that the tribe of Judah was set apart and sanctified for the purpose of praising God.[66]

Delighting in Him and bringing Him joy was literally my strength. Dance was such a part of that expression that I often found myself dancing before Him with complete abandon much like King David did when the Ark of the Covenant was brought into Jerusalem (See 2 Samuel 6). The song, "I will dance like David danced" is a favorite of mine.

> *When the Spirit of the Lord comes upon my heart*
> *I will dance like David danced*
> *When the Spirit of the Lord comes upon my heart*

---

[65]Judah etymology (n.d.). Retrieved from www.abarim-publications.com/Meaning/Judah.html.

[66]The Blessing of Jacob Upon Judah. (Genesis 8-10.)

I will dance like David danced.
I will dance, dance, I will dance like David danced. [67]

My Mentor

The first time I saw Jean Mabry was at Barry Segal's Vision for Israel Conference in Savannah, Georgia. When I saw a group of ladies dancing to the Hebrew song "Jerusalem of Gold" using silk banners and wearing peasant-style outfits, I began to weep for I witnessed the same circle dance I had seen in my mind's eye on the trip down. I spoke to Jean briefly that night but did not comprehend the full impact of her ministry until 1999 when I attended Paul Wilbur's Passover Seder in another town.

I had walked out of the room for a moment and when I returned, a presentation was taking place on stage. When I saw four, 15-foot-long silk banners being billowed in a canopy to Hebraic style music and song, I stopped dead in my tracks. The spectacle was mesmerizing, and I experienced a deeply emotional connection with the spiritual side of the presentation. When I saw the banners being used to magnify and glorify the God of this Universe with dancers flowing in and out from under them, I was filled with a powerful passion to do likewise.

A friend encouraged me to attend a three-day workshop in Columbus, Ohio. I learned how to dye the silks, billow them, and present them in a worship setting. God used Jean Mabry to mentor me for many years. She encouraged me, blessed me with insights regarding the warfare elements of worship in the use of banners (see Isaiah 62:10), and loaned me her silks from time to time.

I came home from that workshop in Ohio, assembled my team, dyed my silks, and gave my first banner presentation at my church in 2002. Jean permitted me to use her choreography ("Let Your Fire Fall"), and after that, I choreographed my dance and banner presentations.

---

[67] Retrieved from http://www.metrolyrics.com/the-spirit-of-david-lyrics-fred-hammond.html.

His Banner Over Me Is Love

How Great Thou Art Banner Presentation
at New Day Church, High Point, NC

The banner ministry was a wonderful and surprising addition to my spiritual life. I created and produced Rivers of Joy Dance and Banner Team under the broader umbrella of Go Thru the Gates Art in Worship Ministry. Both were based on the verse, "Go through, go through the gates! Prepare the way for the people. Cast up, cast up the highway! Gather out the stones. Lift a standard or ensign over and for the peoples" (Isaiah 62:10 AMP).

Eventually, my ministry grew in popularity, and I was asked to present this form of worship during mission conferences, in churches, and other places. For the next eight years, we took the gospel message and God's love through banner presentations into various churches, to Wake Forest University, and to a local men's prison.

When I needed a particular silk banner or set of banners, I either dyed them or bought them from Jean Mabry or Spencer Williams, an artist who created and dyed many of the banners I used. Both of them are founders in the banner ministry and experts in silk artistry. I considered this particular ministry God's special gift to me.

It was a way for Him to communicate with me on a very personal level and a way for me to share that gift with others for inspiration, inner healing, and simple enjoyment.

Glory to the Lamb banner presentation

The following are testimonials regarding *Glory to the Lamb Banner Presentation* at Reynolda Church's "Exalt Him" service in 2006:

> *I have never been so deeply moved by anything before in my entire life. Even after I drove home, tears were still streaming down my face from the emotion of it. God was truly present and all powerful. The joy, love, and contentment, majesty and awe inspired by your presentation is beyond anything I have ever felt.* ~L. Z., Winston-Salem, NC

> *The presence of God was all over your banner presentation. I want to be wherever you give it again, whenever you give it again. I will be talking about this forever.* ~A. D., Winston-Salem, NC.

Judy, know that God is preparing you and using you to prepare others for the coming of our lovely Lord. ~K. R., Winston-Salem, NC.

Judy, truly a work of the Lord! Keep up the good work ~C.S., Clover, SC.

Julie Ann Kimball

At this time in my life, I made a friend so special and precious to me that she will remain my dearest friend forever. Julie came into my life at a Reynolda Women's Retreat. I had been invited to teach a circle dance class and talk about Hebraic art in worship at the Valley Cruzes retreat in 2002. This form of worship so struck her that she sought me out, joined the team, and was at my side from that moment on. The following is a tribute to this special woman of God.

Julie joined the dance team during a performance in honor of David Dolan, who was scheduled to speak at a local church. David is an international speaker, author, commentator, and former CBS news correspondent living in Israel. After the service, Julie and I joined Christian Friends of Israel (CFI) director, Hannele Pardain, and a few others for a private dinner with him. The entire experience gave Julie her first encounter with God's covenant promises to Israel. She was profoundly affected by it, and it was all she talked about on the way home. She kept asking why she had never heard about it before and why the church had never told her about it.

After that, she went with me to Jewish Roots conferences at Montreat, North Carolina, and Barry Segal's Vision for Israel Conferences in Atlanta, Georgia. She hung an Israeli flag outside her house and glued an inscription in Hebrew about praying for Israel in her car. Julie became my permanent partner and special assistant in the banner ministry and performed sacrificially and patiently while running a cleaning business and raising a family.

Banners in the Prison

After that first banner presentation at Reynolda's mission conference, a member of our church on staff at the Cherry Street men's prison in Winston-Salem, North Carolina, approached me and asked me to take the "Let Your Fire Fall" banner presentation into the prison. I said I would think about it but never got back to her due to my fear and reluctance to enter that setting. It took a year or more, a few more presentations, and the Lord's nudging before I got up the courage to do it.

When I met with the director at the prison chapel to get a feel for it, I was told that the prisoners were very polite and that only those who wanted to come would attend. They were not pushed into participating in the Sunday morning services. Because of space limitations, I had to scale everything down and adjust our banners to fit the space given to us. I took Julie Kimball and Scott Brendle with me that first time because they both were willing to go and were experienced in a prison setting. I wasn't as comfortable as they were during our first presentation, but I quickly discovered it to be the most valuable and meaningful part of my banner ministry; it was a spiritual breakthrough for me.

Julie dressed in fire praise garments

During that first presentation, Julie and Scott performed using our lamb and cross banner. They would billow it up and down a few times, then turn it vertically and billow it back and forth before wrapping and unwrapping themselves in it, essentially appearing as pillars wrapped in the blood of the lamb as they presented the banner to Robin Mark's song, "What the Lord Has Done in Me." Some of the words to it are: "Let the weak say I am strong, let the poor say I am rich for what the Lord has done in me."[68] Before this first performance was finished, the CD player went silent during the last verse or two,

---

[68]Listen to "Come Heal This Land" by Robin Marks at https://itunes.apple.com/us/artist/robin-mark/id6596626.

so Julie and Scott immediately began singing the rest of the song while continuing to billow the silk. Then, they floated the banner over the prisoners' heads as they went up and down the aisles. After that first morning, floating the banners over the prisoners became a tradition.

Much later, in another presentation, the Chaplain said that he saw the glory fall on the dove banner we were billowing and the gold flags we were using. He requested we present the routine again at the end of the service.

We had used the Holy Spirit of fire dove banner to billow to the song, "A Resting Place" by Paul Wilbur.[69] The following week I received a call from the Chaplain with a report that the prisoners were saying they felt the wind of the Spirit when the banner passed over their heads. By that time, I had more participants and was blessed beyond measure with no hesitation in interacting with the inmates after the service. But it was Julie and Scott who led the way. I watched them give God's love to those prisoners and freely interact with them.

It was in that prison that the banner team experienced its most treasured and gratifying moments. The Cherry Street men's prison is a minimum-security prison. Most men are there due to low-level drug-related crimes. Our dancers were extremely anointed, extremely modest in their attire. They did nothing to detract from their focus on the Holy Spirit. I believe this is very important in dance ministry.

One of the last presentations we did at the prison was from Chris Tomlin's rendition of "Amazing Grace." I was able to repeat the presentation and to expand it somewhat during a live performance at a local assembly. After the flags and banners were brought in, Anita, our interpretive dancer, came in wearing a scarlet dress over a white praise garment with a black veil covering her head. She used her arm to hide her face as if in shame as she went under the lamb and cross banner and prostrated herself as the banner billowed over her. She then exited the room, shed the crimson and black garments, and returned to the banners wearing a dress and veil of pure white.

---

[69] Listen to "A Resting Place" by Paul Wilber at www.youtube.com/watch?v=BG-wt6EhTq0

A dove banner was then brought in to coincide with the lamb and cross banner. Anita came back in at the appropriate time and danced joyfully in and out of the banners. "Amazing Grace, My Chains Are Gone" by Chris Tomlin[70] was one of the most anointed and powerful dramatic enactments we ever gave using banners, flags, and dance. In the background, Julie and I were on opposite sides, waving rainbow flags representing the promises of God and the colors behind the throne of Revelation 4.

When the prison system changed its format, Sunday morning services stopped in favor of one-on-one contact with the prisoners. Realizing it would be our last time, I brought four videos of various presentations to give to the Chaplain, but the speaker that morning had been so touched by our presentation that I gave the videos to him instead.

Our last presentation was a repeat of "Let Your Fire Fall" by Paul Wilbur. Praise be to God, that small chapel was on fire with all those silks billowings and fire flags waving!

The speaker, a drug dealer who was shot during a drug deal gone bad, said he had never seen anything like it. He was in a wheelchair, paralyzed from the waist down, and part of his correctional sentence was to go into the prison system and share his story with the prisoners.

God's Heart; God's Plan

Once, we experienced a weather-related miracle at the prison before our presentation. I was on my way to meet the team at the church's fellowship hall for us to change into our outfits, but it was raining so hard that the streets were flooding, and I became worried. I knew that the deluge would affect the prison conditions, perhaps we would even have to cancel the service. It would be a long walk through the prison yard to the Chapel, which meant our banners and praise garments would get soaked. While driving to the church praying about the situation, suddenly the Holy Spirit rose mightily in me. I experienced a powerful anointing to speak directly to the

---

[70]Listen to "Amazing Grace, My Chains are Gone" by Chris Tomlin at www.youtube.com/watch?v=Y-4NFvI5U9w

weather to command it to stop raining. I was taken aback at this and didn't dare to do it at first, but I knew God was giving me the unction to pray more than a simple, "please stop raining" type of prayer. Thus, after a bit of Holy Ghost nudging, I opened my mouth and spoke to the elements. I sent out a prayer of faith with such passion that I surprised myself. My Lord was speaking to the firmament through me. Let us not forget that there was biblical support for this when Jesus said to them, "Have faith in God [constantly]. Truly I tell you, whoever says to this mountain, be lifted up and thrown into the sea and does not doubt at all in his heart, but believes that what he says will take place, it will be done for him" (Mark 11:23 AMP).

However, the rain continued to pour while I unloaded the car at the Fellowship Hall, but by the time we arrived at the prison, the sun was shining! What a mighty God we serve! We ended up trekking through the courtyard beside the building housing the prisoners instead of entering through a side door to the chapel. I felt many eyes on us as we marched through the middle of their prison yard dressed in gold. Later, one inmate spoke up and told us that he was not going to come to the service, but when he looked out his window and saw angels walking past him in the courtyard, he was compelled to come. What a blessing to get to be part of such a ministry.

Chapel attendance by the inmates is voluntary so only a certain percentage of the prison population attended Sunday morning services. I found out later that if there had been heavy rain, inmates would have remained in their rooms since their route would have caused them to get drenched by walking from their cell to the chapel

Spontaneous worship: Julie dancing for joy in the courtyard after our first presentation at the men's prison.

building. The minister who was to speak that morning was delayed due to the flood-like conditions across town in her area. Only in our area, only at the prison location, had the deluge stopped.

The only picture I have from the prison ministry was spontaneously taken when I saw Julie Kimball dancing in the parking lot outside the prison. We couldn't take a camera inside, so I snapped the photo in a moment of triumph and praise for the success of our ministry work there that morning.

Julie's Servanthood

After I returned from each overseas missionary trip and before each class began, my precious friend would gather chairs around the floor in front of the stage so the dancers could hear all about my mission trips.

I remember the day when she told me her maiden name was *Julie Ann Frank*. I knew she was watching my face and especially my eyes, as she gauged my reaction, and I am sure it was exactly as she expected. I was visibly impacted and practically stuttered, "But, but...that's Jewish!"

She told me that the Franks left Germany before the Holocaust and never admitted to having any ties to the Jews. I realize now that this was a thread, the case for spiritual-legal ground through her generational lineage. Her love (phylo-Semitism) for Israel flowed directly from her ancestors, providing (precedent) for her love of Hebraic style worship dance and banners.

Julie had a servant's heart with the gift of "helps" (administration). She went before and behind me, always making sure the banners and dance outfits were properly hung and packed by the various team members. God was bringing Julie into His special, divine calling to glorify and worship Him through dance and with banners.

During our presentation at Wake Forest University Scales Fine Arts Center, she had a stomach virus. The other team members had to pick her up from lying on the floor just before her routine. Miraculously, she performed her dance beautifully and without incident. Afterward, she collapsed and was immediately taken home. But she refused to leave until she told a team member, "Take care of Judy. Make sure she gets help in packing up and taking things to her car." This was no small job since I had many costumes and praise garments as well as banners and banner poles.

On another occasion, Julie washed the feet of our entire worship team. In 2003, I was about to participate in an inter-denominational musical drama. Julie had commitments and could not be part of it, but a few days before we were to present the program, she called saying God had told her to wash the feet of all those participating. Obediently, she drove 40 miles each way to the church with a beautiful ceramic pitcher, a basin, and a towel. She went from one individual to another, pouring warm water over their feet and, while washing them, spoke a personal blessing to each one. She did not even know many of these people. What an example of pure servanthood that was to each of us!

On the day of the dress rehearsal for this same drama, I was in my garage standing on a step ladder, painting the last of three floor-to-ceiling length panels to be used as backdrops. I knew I had only a few hours to finish, and time was running out. The desert scene was not progressing well. I had a huge mess confronting me that needed to be painted over, but I had run out of white acrylic paint. I needed it desperately. The level of stress on me at that moment was enormous. At that precise moment, Julie came driving up with her little girl, Laura Grace, to see how I was doing. She saw the disaster on canvas, and calmly said, "What can I do to help?" When I told her about the paint, she said, "I'll go get some." That was not a simple task since the nearest art supply store was miles away. Nevertheless, she went into town and returned a short time later with a huge tube of white paint, then left me alone to finish. I made the correction and finished the panels in the nick of time. The production team never knew what Julie did for us that day.

Goodbye Julie

Once, during the early years of the banner ministry, when I was teaching circle dance classes, a woman came occasionally to join in the dance. She supported our banner and dance ministry but never danced in a formal presentation with us. One night after class, she approached me with a concern she had because of a prophetic word she claimed to have been given. She thought she had a word of knowledge about someone on the team. As she spoke, tears welled up in her eyes. She said she was receiving something about a member of my banner team who had "attached herself" to the ministry. Her tears of sadness conveyed that something terrible was going to happen, but she did not give voice to it.

For years after this unusual occurrence, I wondered what it was that God had imparted to her. She seemed to indicate that she either didn't have a full understanding or did not want to tell me. After that, I contemplated who it might be. Was it the woman with an occult background who had joined the team? Would she inadvertently (through past associations and belief structures) harm the team effort? In time, I had to replace this individual, but my heart told me that Julie was the only one who had attached herself to my banner ministry. Not having the prophetic insight in full was perplexing, but when the ministry thrived, I pushed it to the back of my mind.

Today, I know that the terrible thing she saw was Julie's death. Julie Ann Frank Kimball died of ovarian cancer in 2011. She had surgery for ovarian cancer in 2002, and we believed she had been healed, but seven years later, it came back.

She accompanied me to Dr. Howard and Janet Morgan's Panim El Panim conference in 2009, but by that time, she had no hair left due to the chemotherapy treatments she had endured. She wore a scarf over her head after abandoning attempts to wear a wig. I learned from her why most cancer patients do not wear wigs—without hair, a wig is very uncomfortable. It becomes hot and itchy, and it won't stay in place.

When Julie went into the hospital for the final time, I emailed a few photos of her to a mutual dance friend. She printed them and gave them to the hospital Chaplain who plastered them all over her room in those final days. I have many photos of Julie performing in the banner ministry and will never forget how beautiful she was when engaged in spontaneous and joyous worship. She was like a child in expressing her joy and exuberance. The following is a letter I wrote and shared with her a few weeks before she passed away.

Dear Julie,
When a treasured friend suffers, this heart cries.
When comfort, peace, and rest no longer abide, this heart cries.
When a soul is robbed of its joy, this heart cries.
Come, Lord Jesus. Now is the time. Heal and deliver. Now is the time. Let us see your face. Now is the time. My heart calls upon your promises. Now is the time. Bind up the brokenhearted. Now is the time.

Such a friend, who can fathom? If not for you, Hebraic dance and banners would not have happened. If not for you, my heart's desire and dream would still be roaming around, out there somewhere, finally to die. If not for you, those men in prison would not have tasted A Resting Place, Holy Fire, and Amazing Grace. If there ever was such a thing as wind beneath one's wings, you are that.

I look forward to dancing with you again. I look forward to waving flags and to billow those banners with you again. You are a precious treasure, a jewel in God's kingdom. He loves you, and I love you, and that's the way it's gonna be. Forever.

Your forever friend,
Judy

Father's Waiting Arms

Many believe the veil between this life and the next becomes thinner when a loved one passes away or is about to pass away. I experienced this when my dear Moravian Pastor Helmich died. It is then that supernatural phenomena has been known to occur. On September 26, 2011, at 4:00 in the morning, I experienced one such phenomenon in the form of a vision. It came to me in different shapes, and except for one, the objects were purple in the center with a gold perimeter against a black background. The golden perimeter looked like liquefied gold; it was both solid and liquid with overlapping cone-like shapes, all having points resembling teeth of varying lengths that were pointing outward, away from the center. They were terrifying.

When the vision first began to form, two round objects were mirror images of each other. The teeth-like edges of uneven length gave the centers the appearance of open chasms or passageways that I could not see through. There were four scenes in all; each remained for a few seconds before changing into another shape. Some shapes looked like female reproductive organs.

In the last vision, I saw a set of lungs, ashen gray, and death-like in appearance against a dark gray background. Just below them and in the center was a round object, the color of purple and gold mixed with red. It was covered with a mist, making it look less intense than it would have otherwise. The lungs were fading out as the final image dissipated.

I asked God for interpretation, and I heard the word "portal" and then "portals of heaven." I immediately thought of my friend, Julie, lying in a hospital bed, enduring the final stages of ovarian cancer. Was God's hand reaching down through a portal to heal her at that very moment, or was He reaching down to take her home? Was she being healed, or was she dying?

I did not know. I could not go back to sleep, so I got up and drew what I had seen. The visions appeared during that twilight period between being awake and drifting off to sleep. I wasn't asleep. I wasn't dreaming. The images were very sharp and clear. I remembered them well.

The fact that the first two shapes were mirror images of each other puzzled me. It pricked my imagination and encouraged my spirit to seek revelation. I pondered it, put it on my "pantry shelf" to study and ask for understanding.

And God answered my prayer. First, He reminded me that it was not the first time I had seen mirror images of each other. The other time was after the death of Hassell, my husband's uncle, at his funeral. I noted the time of this new vision–4:00 am on Monday, September 26, 2011. I headed out of town the next day, and upon my return, I learned that Julie had gone into a coma and died that day.

I received the interpretation of this vision right after Julie's funeral. The pale gray, ashen-colored lungs represented death, while the round heart shape below it meant –life not yet extinguished (she was still living at the time I received the vision). The mirror images represented two wombs; one was natural and the other supernatural. The reproductive organs in the second and third visions represented the birthing process.

Metaphorically speaking, God's children pass through the mother's birth canal before entering this world. When it is time for them to depart this world, His children enter the portals of heaven through a similar but supernatural birthing process. When children are born in the natural, they immediately go into the waiting arms of their mother. In the heavenly realm, the born again go immediately into the waiting arms of their Father.

In the vision, I was seeing Julie's spirit and soul in transition. The red and purple colors in the object below her lungs represented royalty and purity through the blood of Jesus. She was the daughter of the King, purified and perfect, able to stand before her Father cleansed through the shed blood of Jesus. But the jagged edges making up the perimeter of the images was most intimidating, awesome, and frightening. I believe they represented divine protection while God's children are passing through heavenly portals from this world to the next.

None of us know when our time here on earth will end, and we step through the portals of heaven, but I can tell you without a shadow of a doubt when Julie stepped into heaven, she was dancing the dance of her life in her Father's presence, so utterly happy and free from pain.

Julie Ann Kimball, this chapter is dedicated to you.

His Banner Over Me Is Love

Part IV

Missions:
From Jamaica To Auschwitz

CHAPTER 14

JAMAICA SETS THE STAGE

Seeing the Need for Missions

God launched me into missions in 1997 when I asked to be part of a mission trip to Jamaica with my church's building and medical team. Jamaica is an island in the West Indies under the British Crown and has a substantial tourist trade, but it is also a country of poverty and despair and in great need of missions. There is a strong oppressive spirit over Jamaica that came through the historical atrocities of the slave trade and pirate activity, and it continues through occult religions and the thriving drug trade.

Tourists who go there quickly discover that it is very different from other islands in the Caribbean. For example, the beautiful hotels rimming the coast offer paradise's delusion in an otherwise harsh, brutal environment. Food is a constant problem, and water is critical for the natives. Large reservoirs can be seen atop most private dwellings to catch rainwater, but tourists are shielded by the amenities lavished upon them at the Jamaican hotels. It is only when they attempt to leave the hotel compounds that they come face to face with the reality of living in Jamaica. Ship captains routinely warn tourists against leaving the tour group for any reason.

One ship captain shared a tale of two women who did not listen. They hired a taxi driver to take them to the beach, and the driver took their money and their clothes, leaving them stranded, naked, and alone on a remote beach.

We flew to Jamaica to work with Teamwork Associates Christian School outside Montego Bay. Pastor Menzie Oban, the principal operator of this school, left his vocation as a sheet metal engineer, sacrificing his personal success to answer God's call to ministry. While training at an Assemblies of God Bible School in England, he became involved in the ministry of the late Derek Prince and answered a divine calling to come back to his home country and start this school. I am a dental hygienist by profession, so my skills were much needed. I found myself cleaning teeth, educating school children, washing dishes, serving food, and once leading a morning devotion.

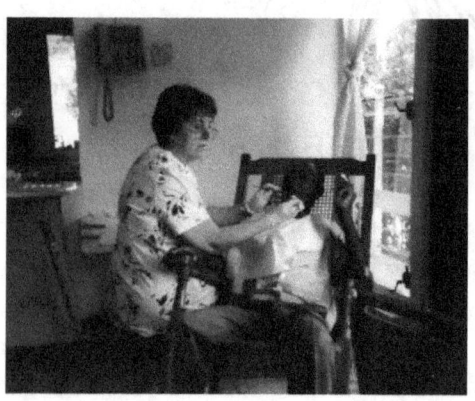

1997 | Judy cleaning teeth in Jamaica

Teamwork Associates currently functions as a school, a church, and a retreat center. In 1997, it was a lighthouse on a hill, sitting atop a mountain of spiritual darkness. On our time off, we traveled to Ochre Rios, swam in the Caribbean briefly, visited Dunwoody Falls, and at each place, the natives mostly looked at us with distrust, some with what felt like hatred in their eyes. They were aggressive in their manner and attitude toward us, but at the Christian school, the Spirit of the Lord was strong. The driver who picked us up at the airport was a joyous young fellow who had been delivered from a life of drugs after an encounter with Jesus Christ through the ministry of Menzie Oban.

All of the leaders and teachers at the school were born-again, Spirit-filled Christians who interceded for their fellow Jamaicans. Late at night, I could hear prayer meetings taking place on the floor below us in the teacher's quarters.

There was no mistaking the sound coming from the move of the Holy Spirit among this small band of intercessors. Several years later, one of them moved to America, became part of our congregation,

Jamaica Sets the Stage

and participated in two of my banner presentations. It was a joy to see Sylvia wear her native Jamaican dress during my flag presentations to the song "We Speak to Nations."[71] During that mission fundraiser at my church, each of us wore native costumes that represented each country supported by Reynolda's full-time missionaries. Hearing this song by Israel Houghton still brings tears to my eyes.

Some of our team brought salvation and demonic deliverance to one of the young boys who camped out on the property behind the school. Approximately 10 to 15 youths ranging in age from 15 to 17 years old had no place else to go except the streets or the drug trade. They were allowed a haven on the property and would show up to greet us each afternoon. No one was allowed in the dorm where we stayed at any time for any reason, but learning that we liked ripe bananas instead of the boiled green ones served in the cafeteria, they gathered a bunch of ripe ones, brought them to the entrance to the dorm and offered them to us. When I returned to my room after a prayer meeting one night, my roommate had placed a single ripe banana on my bed. I devoured it. It was the best-tasting banana I had eaten.

Much of the food consumed at the school was grown on the grounds. They raised their own chickens and since my husband's hobby was beekeeping, I was most interested in seeing the beehives on their property.

Due to extreme poverty, everything that the land gave to the natives had to be reserved for those with the money to buy it. I found that the fresh fruits I had expected to enjoy in this tropical environment were actually scarce on the island because the poor farmers needed to sell them to the cruise ships and hotels for money to support their families. All the delicious fruits and vegetables were rationed even for the school children. We had about one-fourth of pineapple at each meal along with a portion of chicken that was mostly bones, and at breakfast, I never knew if I was eating real scrambled eggs or a certain fruit that looked and tasted like eggs. A native fruit from Africa, it is grown on the island and is a staple

---

[71] Listen to "We Speak to Nations" on: www.youtube.com/watch?v=c4qH3PfyTlo.

in the Jamaican diet. It is called Ackee, but if eaten too soon, it is poisonous. For lunch, my roommate, Cheryl, and I usually opted to remain in our room when they served chicken feet soup. Cheryl and I met in Susan Miller's Bible study class prior to the trip, but in Jamaica, we got to know each other well. Cheryl eventually became a full-time missionary in another country.

One day at dusk, Cheryl and I were walking back to our dorm room when we came face to face with a day worker on his way home. He was riding his bicycle and much to our surprise, he stopped and began to talk to us. We didn't know whether to listen or flee. It had been difficult looking at this man and most challenging to talk to him. He had lost the sight in his eye from a machete knife during a fight. His job was chopping up chicken, and he would only glance at us workers in the kitchen without speaking.

The little ray of sunshine, my friend Susan had pushed through this man's shyness and engaged him in conversation. From that, I learned a few things about him. He was the son of migrant workers traveling the cane fields, and like Gypsies, his family lived in a caravan on the move from one field to the next.

I sensed that he was a man coming from a realm of oppressive darkness but beginning to encounter real Christian love during his contact with the school. It was clear that he did not know how to reciprocate such unconditional love, but it was also apparent that he was trying. I prayed that this man's journey in life would continue to carry him to that school and to the Savior.

One night, a local man visited our nightly gatherings in the cafeteria. He told us that he had been on his way to kill a man, but he was in such distress about it that he stopped at a local church service. When he went in, he got saved, gave up his weapon, and found his way to Teamwork Associates lighthouse on a hill.

In Jamaica, my roommate and I fully came to understand the need for missions. God turned a key in the door of both our hearts. Cheryl went home, sold her spacious home, bought a smaller one, and began to focus her entire life toward missions.

I, on the other hand, have a different story to tell. Sitting outside my dorm room, studying the flickering lights from the cruise ships, I reflected upon the reason and need for missions.

Jamaica Sets the Stage

I pondered the realm between light and darkness and the difference between the two theologies I grew up with: one that saw no need for missions and one that did.

Primitive Baptists reject missionary efforts. The need for missions was the primary reason for the split between the two denominational assemblies I grew up in. Before going to Jamaica, God put the desire for missions in my heart, then created the circumstances by which fruition of that desire came into being. He called, and I answered. I stepped out in faith knowing full well I would get no support from my parents. I stepped out in faith, trusting God to work in the heart of my husband, to agree to that mission trip and those that followed. Glory to God! My parents remained loyal in their love and support. My mother told a friend from her church how proud she was of me. Love found a way—and Jamaica set the stage that led me to God's ultimate purpose for my life.

CHAPTER 15

MISSION TRIP TO ENGLAND

Hyde Park, 1998

I was thrilled when I was given the opportunity to participate in a new mission endeavor. This one would take me to London, and I had one day to make my decision. The mission was to be an evangelistic outreach to Londoners and the myriad of tourists visiting the city daily. I was grateful to be a part of it. We were scheduled to partner with England's London City Missions (LCM). One of its pastors, Julio, originally from Zimbabwe, was our contact minister and host. I was scheduled to participate in street witnessing, house to house evangelism, and various mission endeavors throughout London, including outreaches at several Christ Churches and evangelism in Hyde Park. I had never done these things, and when I found out what I would be expected to do, I fasted for two weeks. Fear of the unknown is a powerful tool of the devil, and it is at those times when faith in God's power to get you through can make all the difference.

When I first met everyone who would be a part of the mission group, I was amazed to recognize a familiar face. Jeanette Hartley was my uncle's first cousin, whom I had met in my childhood. This most unusual and powerful woman of God took me under her wing as we walked together by the Spirit on that trip. It was Jeanette who urged me to go on other short-term mission trips.

We would pray, "Lord, give us more. Give us more missions." And He did! Over a million tourists walk the streets of London on any given day. We handed out gospel tracts, which wound up in the hands of individuals from other countries and the locals, making it a cross-cultural evangelistic experience for me. We stayed at the Vandon House Hotel, a Salvation Army Bed and Breakfast located only two blocks from Buckingham Palace. Jamaica was challenging for me, but the demands of this trip proved far greater because its thrust was so different. It required direct evangelism.

Medical and building missionary efforts are indirect because they require the use of certain skills, including purely physical labor. In Jamaica, I was expected to share God's love through my dental hygiene skills and talk to the children about how much God loves them without evangelizing them while my hands were in their mouths. Engaging strangers on the streets, testifying in churches, and evangelizing house to house require completely different skills. But we were prepared. We spent a day under LCM's council before being assigned to one of their ministers and taking to the streets.

London City Missions

LCM is an outreach comprised of individual ministers assigned to various sections of London according to their special gifting and calling. On our first dy there, we met with an LCM trainer, a German gentleman named Bernard, who explained our mission and how we should approach the English. I was assigned to partner with him at Tower Hill while we passed out tracts to tourists on

1998 | London City Mission

vacation. The Tower Hill Bridge, connecting North and South London, is often mistaken for the older and more famous London Bridge.

Bernard's command of the German language enabled him to talk to a group of German boys 10-12 years of age who were passing through Tower Hill. These children were taught evolution in school and did not believe in God; they believed they evolved from apes. Though I could not understand the language, there was no mistaking the angry retort from one of the boys. At one point, Bernard turned to me and said in English, "This young man says there is no God. What is your answer to him?"

The answer I gave to an obviously belligerent adolescent was not apologetic or scripted. What came out of my mouth was a testimony. I said, "I know there is a God because I know Him and have a personal relationship with Him." After Bernard translated, the boy did not respond, but his body language and facial expression told me he had no framework for comprehending or receiving what I was talking about. The key to unlocking that young boy's heart and understanding was not in my hands. I could only pray that God had planted a seed through me. Just after that encounter, I gave a tract to a young German girl. Her mother immediately yanked it from her hand and tossed it on the ground, but it warmed my heart when another family, seeing what had happened, walked up to me and said, "We want you to know that we are German and we love Jesus."

1998 | Judy testifying at Christ Church

French schoolchildren passing through Tower Hill were open, friendly, and receptive. LCM told us that less than 2 percent of French families own Bibles.

I participated in open-air night missions at Leicester Square. My partner was a young LCM intern named Jim. My job was to hand out tracts, and if the opportunity arose, engage people in conversation about Jesus Christ. Jim set up an easel and began to paint what looked like a bunch of blank squares against a black background, and by the time he finished, the picture revealed the words "Jesus Saves." The art was successful because it drew a crowd of curious onlookers with whom I could talk to and pass out tracts.

Moments before we were about to leave, an old gentleman approached us. He was looking at the finished artwork intently while twisting his hat in his hands. I walked up to him and asked if he was a Christian to which he replied, "I thought I was until today when I got into an argument with my Pastor." He indicated that he was unsure of his salvation and wondered if he had lost it altogether. Suddenly, as he trembled before me, God revealed that he had a heart hungry for the gospel truth and was ready to receive it.

The content (gospel message), the medium (one who delivers the message), and the receptor (the heart ready to receive) merged instantly at that moment. I called Jim over, and together we led this old gentleman in the sinner's prayer to receive the Lord Jesus Christ as his personal Savior with the assurance of his salvation. Earlier that morning, these elements were not in place when Bernard and I spoke to the German youth, but I believe we laid the groundwork for another to build on.

A few days later, in one of London's many Christ Churches, I was asked to give my testimony. Our team leader, Len Brown, turned to me and asked me to speak just moments before entering the church. I was totally unprepared and not good at that sort of thing.

Doing It Afraid

I felt like I died a thousand deaths from that moment on until I was called up to speak. Fear clutched at me, but once I started talking, I found I did not want to stop! As I searched my mind for what I was to say, the only thing that came into my spirit was my testimony, so I talked about what happened to me at the altar of the Moravian church 26 years before. After the service, the pastor came up to me and said that this congregation was comprised of members from the Calvinist Presbyterian Church in Scotland, and what I said was exactly what they needed to hear. I am not sure what he meant by that, but I knew that given the fact that I told them about how God supernaturally unshackled me from the bonds of my self-righteousness and despair over where I would spend eternity and assured me of my salvation, this congregation knew where I was coming from. They were of the same religious soil as I, and judging from the Pastor's remarks, I believe my testimony handed him the key to unlocking some previously locked doors.

Len told me later that he had sprung it on me deliberately and suddenly so that I would cast myself wholly on the Lord and not rely on my strength and mental ability. It worked. But I came close to hyperventilating during those first few moments before getting up to speak. Jeanette and my other teammate, prayed for me while I sat there, barely breathing and crying out to God for Him to give me something to say.

Because I had no time to choose the subject matter, what came forth did not come from my own fleshly waters but from the Holy Spirit's clear flowing waters. I had never spoken before about what had happened to me at the altar of Hopewell Moravian Church. Amazingly, it took the crisis of the moment to bring it out. I didn't know it then, but a hidden thread from my past joined forces with God's Holy Spirit to produce living waters at King's Cross Church in North London.

Legal Ground

About mid-week, we had one hour of free time in a shopping mall. I made a beeline to the nearest jewelry store, determined to buy a necklace. I wanted something Jewish like the Star of David or a Menorah, but all they had was the Hebrew letter for L'Chaim, meaning *"to life"* in English. Having seen *Fiddler on the Roof*, I immediately knew what it was and its significance. I was ecstatic to find it and wore it proudly when I went into Hyde Park. The morning we were to go into the park, we participated in another Christ Church service, at which time a man came up to me and said, "I hear you are going into Hyde Park this afternoon. I want you to know that my father preached the gospel there for many years, so you have *legal ground*." I did not understand it then, but this man's words became a marvelous confession and turned out to be predictive of personal encounters some of us had in the Park that day. For me, it revealed another hidden thread. I believe that because of it, I stepped into a divine appointment. I had never heard of the term before, but the concept of the spiritual-legal ground became very significant in later years. It helped me understand much about my life both retroactively and going forward.

Hostile Place

Before my trip to London, I came under the teaching of a prominent evangelist who said that Hyde Park is one of the two most hostile places in the world to preach the gospel. True or not, it filled me with misgivings and dread of the place. Street witnessing was brand new to me. I had been amazed and tremendously encouraged by how the Lord had used me as an intercessor for Jeanette as she interacted with many to receive the Lord, including the Holy Ghost baptism of Fire.

I cherish the memory of street evangelism and my Christ Church experiences, but on this day, I was apprehensive about what I might encounter in the Park. Fresh in my mind were reports of hostile encounters, including a Bible being thrown at an LCM pastor, so I was dragging my feet and grumbling to myself as I approached the entrance to the "Speaker's Corner." I thought, why go? We can't make a difference here. Given a choice, I would have easily turned around and went back.

Many times my obedience meant walking *not by sight nor by might but by His Spirit*. The Spirit of faith moved me and, at times, was filled with fear and trembling. The flesh can do that. A Sunday school teacher once talked about her fear of public speaking. The title of her message was, "Do it afraid." Many times my path entailed

Mission Trip to England

"doing it afraid." Taking one step, then another in faith, often brought surprise and jubilation over what the Lord did in me and through me. Sometimes it was done despite me. Covering fresh new ground, especially in the early years of my ministry, was never easy. Hyde Park was like that. But praise God, London was a proving ground, setting the stage for future mission outreaches.

We were headed that day into the section of the Park called the *Speaker's Corner*. In this corner of the Park, anyone can say anything they want to say to the public at large, but just like in America, the speaker has to provide a stool, called a bandbox, to stand upon while addressing the public. Preaching was Julio's job, while the team hung around to support him and talk to people about the gospel.

As I wandered around, I stumbled upon a team member talking to a man wearing the Star of David and a Menorah around his neck. We had ridden through a Jewish neighborhood earlier in the week, and every time I saw Hassidic Jews (a specific sect of Jews) walking on the sidewalks, something burned inside me. I wanted to connect with someone from the Jewish community during the trip, but I knew it would be next to impossible in my heart since we were going into Hyde Park on the very last day of our mission journey.

My hopes had all but disappeared when I heard this tall, middle-aged, Jewish man saying, "I believe in binding and loosing." Since I had never heard anyone but a Charismatic using that biblical phrase "binding and loosing," my heart leaped at the chance to meet what appeared to be a born again Jewish believer and a spirit-filled one at that! I went right up to him with a wide grin and began jingling my necklace in front of him. To my delight, he smiled back and said, "Ahhhh, L'Chaim, to life!"

His name was Joseph Ben-Israel (not his real name), and as soon as I met him, my love for Israel and the Jewish people began pouring forth from my heart. I couldn't seem to stop myself. He felt that love, and like a dam bursting; started sharing details about his torturous childhood. He told me he was urinated upon, raped, and abused just because he was Jewish. He spoke about being the only child of Holocaust survivors. It was a miracle he was even born because of the sexual experimentation performed on his parents by the evil Nazi doctor, Josef Mengele, the famous "Angel of Death."

I received a copy of Joseph's written testimony with details of his conversion. Interestingly, his conversion came about after a Christian saw him in the Jewish section of a library and noticing his appearance, asked, "Are you a Jew?" At the time, Joseph's appearance identified him as an ultra-orthodox Jew, so he said sarcastically, "Who do you think I am?" Not understanding why this man was in the Jewish section of the library, hatred rose in Joseph like bile, and he unleashed it upon the stranger. He told about the abuse his parents had suffered at the hands of German Christians and the antisemitism he had experienced from Christians.

This Gentile Christian man, who was there to learn more about things Jewish, exclaimed, "Just because you put a horse in a garage, doesn't make it a car. Just because one labels himself a Christian doesn't make him one. The Nazis were not Christians. Any torture you received in the name of Christianity because you are Jewish did not come from Christians. I am a Christian. I love Jews, and I am trying to reconnect to my Jewish roots—to the original chosen people of God." So...because this born again, Protestant Christian persevered to the extent that what began as an angry, antagonistic meeting ended up with Joseph beginning to understand true Christianity.

He accepted an invitation to the man's church and was soon born again in his Messiah Yeshua/Jesus. When his parents found out about it, they had a funeral for him. To them, he was no longer a Jew. To them, he had joined the religious organization that had persecuted, tortured, and murdered their people for hundreds of years.

The pain of remembering the Holocaust and what the Nazis did to his family created trouble for Joseph. He had experienced his Savior's love for Gentiles, but he could not rid himself of the hatred he felt for the Austrians and the Germans. Finally, one night, he fell to his knees and cried out to God to change his heart and take away the hatred that was eating him up and destroying his peace. That night he slept peacefully, and the next morning, the hatred was gone. The Lord took it from him and replaced it with a kind of love that Joseph had never known. God then told him to take this love to the Austrians and the Germans.

Linz, Austria

That day in Hyde Park, he told me that he was preparing to go into Linz, Austria, the birthplace of Adolf Hitler. He had been invited to meet with the Austrian Christians to encourage them to stand up to their government about destroying Hitler's birthplace, for it had become a gathering place for neo-Nazis.

After this amazing encounter, I asked Joseph Ben-Israel if I could pray for him. He agreed as long as I would allow him to pray for me afterward. I put my hand on his shoulder and began to pray, and as I did so, I felt an electrical current begin to course through his body.

He began to sway back and forth. Then, he prayed for me, and we exchanged addresses. When he turned around, we saw a group of teenage boys ranging in ages from 15 to 17 approaching. He faced the group, stretched out his arms, and began telling them about the love of Jesus. He explained how Jesus had transformed his life and said how, as a Jew, he had hated all Gentiles until Jesus saved him and gave him a love for all people. Then he asked where they were from and when they said, "Linz, Austria," I thought, "God, what are You doing? I am going to stay and watch this!" The teenagers expressed indifference but stayed to listen to Joseph's testimony. Amazingly, they did not walk off though one of them gave a hand gesture that seemed to say, "So what, who cares?"

As soon as Joseph finished, I stepped into that semi-circle of young people, held up a cassette tape, and said, "I am an American. If you want to know more about what the power of God can do in a person's life, this is a testimony of a woman kidnapped by a serial killer in Texas. While he was preparing to kill her, she talked to him about the gospel of Jesus Christ and instead of killing her, he stopped the car, threw his hands in the air and asked God to forgive him.

The power of God fell on him, and he was born again in Jesus Christ. After a pregnant pause, the same boy who had made the hand gesture reached out and took the cassette tape from me. Almost immediately, I felt the anointing for this encounter leave me. I turned to Joseph Ben-Israel said goodbye, and rejoined the team.

I walked out of Hyde Park that day fueled with a fresh love for Israel, the Jewish people, and the friendship of a Messianic Jewish man. When I got home, I received a postcard from him, postmarked from Linz, Austria, with a picture of Hitler's birthplace at Branau Am Inn on the front. We have kept in touch through the years through cards posted from various countries affected by the Holocaust. God gave me the desire of my heart to meet this Jewish man that day in Hyde Park.

I left London with a strange new concept that took many years to uncover the meaning of, build upon, and realize its significance. Once visible, a generational thread slowly began to unravel and reveal itself in understanding the term *"legal ground."* The tape I gave to the youth in Hyde Park contained the incredible true account of Margy Mayfield. The same Spirit who flowed through Margy to reach the man who was about to kill her is the same Holy Spirit of God who flows directly into the hearts of those listening to her story. It is an awesome, articulate rendering of the gospel message to anyone who has never heard about Jesus Christ and just as powerful to those who have. The taped testimony of this amazing woman flows directly into another one just as amazing.

Chapter 16

Rejection, Redemption, and the River of Life

The Story of Hassell

Hassell, my husband's favorite uncle, lived to be 94 years old. Claiming to be an atheist, he was completely unresponsive to the gospel. He was an avid reader and knew quite a lot about many subjects. On one of my last visits with him, he was rambling on about science and evolution. He even shared his knowledge about the chemical makeup of the serving table beside his bed at the nursing home.

When he went into the nursing home suffering from heart failure, we all knew his time was short. As it turned out, I only had two visits with him before he passed away. On our first visit, I gave him one of my Bibles after carefully inserting tiny pieces of paper to serve as bookmarks on pages containing verses about our need for a Savior and how to be saved. I sat by Hassell's bed while my husband and a friend were visiting in a far corner of the room. He brushed away my efforts to give him the Bible by saying, "I have five just like them at home." So, I put it on the bookcase behind him and said no more about it.

Then when he began to talk, I just listened, making few, if any, comments. Since I had prayed prior to this visit for God to give me an opportunity to speak to him about where he would spend eternity, I knew God had this; I just had to wait.

Hassell kept on rambling but periodically came back to the topic of God and salvation. He downplayed the crucifixion by saying it was only a popular Roman method of execution at the time, as if that explained it. Slowly, I began to see a pattern emerging about Jesus and the cross. So I thought to myself, the next time he brings this up, I am not going to keep silent; I am going to jump in. Sure enough, the subject rolled around again, and I told him that Jesus was destined to die specifically during the Roman era because God planned it that way. I told him that Christ's death on a Roman cross was the method by which He was to become the sacrificial lamb, thereby fulfilling the prophecy of Isaiah 53.

Then, when the topic migrated to his belief in science and evolution, I said. "That's fine. Just don't make it your religion." I explained that expressing blind faith in something that has not been proven as fact can be defined as religion because if you substitute science and evolution for a theological belief in God, it becomes theological in nature and, therefore, a religion.

Hassell was a seeker of knowledge, educating himself well beyond the level of a master's degree on various subjects such as chemistry, electronics, history, and politics. His home was filled with hundreds of books. He had read every one and could converse on any subject matter. He had a chemistry lab (from his early childhood years) in a back room that needed to be disposed of after his death. I heard that once his experiments caused a mini-explosion. When the remains of all his test tubes still filled with chemicals were found, a government agency had to be called in to dispose of them.

He continued talking in a circular fashion about subjects having to do with science then back again to spiritual matters. This time he raised his forefinger, pointed it into the air and said, "When I was a child, people would shake their finger at me and say, 'If you don't join the church and be baptized, you are going to hell.'" Aha! I recognized the offense! Immediately, upon hearing him say this, I took his hand and told him it was not what he did but what Jesus did for him that mattered. All he had to do was to believe it—to place his faith in it. It was a matter of the heart. [Offense in any realm, but especially in the realm of the Spirit, is the bait (tool) of Satan because it provides fertile ground for the enemy to bring disillusionment and loss of faith to God's people and the church as a whole.

Hassell was in a wheelchair, and during this part of the conversation, I was bending over him, still holding his hand. Suddenly he became emotional and started to cry. Then, just as suddenly, he drew himself up and said, emphatically, "You're trying to convert me, and you're not going to!" With that, the conversation ended.

By this time, two hours had passed, the friend in the room had left, and my husband rescued me by saying it was time to go. The following week, I took Hassell my home-made blonde brownies, his favorite, a written report of my personal testimony, and the cassette tape of Margy Mayfield placed inside a hand-held tape recorder. The brownies were a peace offering. The testimony was a witness about my supernatural encounter with Christ at Hopewell Moravian Church. No one can argue with a testimony; they either receive it or not. To my surprise, when I saw him that day, he extended his arm toward the Bible on his shelf, repeatedly saying, "I tell people about your Bible." I made no comment, and the subject of religion never came up. The last time I saw him, he was holding the tape player and my testimony. As my husband and I were leaving, I turned to look back at him one last time. I will forever cherish his parting words to me. He said, "I like you. I have always liked you."

I thought we would have one more visit with him before he passed, but it was not to be. Hassell died a week later. The funeral consisted of a graveside service. I recall very little of what the preacher said except his opening statement, "I can't tell you where Hassell is right now. We had many long talks about religion when I visited him at the nursing home, but that was as far as it went." After that honest and caring remark, he proceeded to give the eulogy.

I was seated in the front row facing the casket when I saw someone helping his sister, in her nineties, to her seat. I was overcome with emotion, so I shut my eyes, and when I did, I had a strange, compelling vision. At first, I thought I saw images of the distant trees.

I opened my eyes and closed them several times, but the vision remained. It began as disjointed images that came together like pieces of a puzzle. Suddenly, I knew it was not trees I was seeing.

There appeared before me two horizontal, linear objects that were mirror images of each other. The ends facing each other were bulbous while the stems were tubular. The color was a vibrant, translucent, emerald green that seemed to flow within the shapes and through one shape to the other. The bulbous ends were expanding and contracting. They were repeatedly pulsating like a balloon does when squeezed. As we left the gravesite that day, I said to myself, "What in the world was that? I will never know the meaning of that!"

I pondered what God was showing me for months, but it made no sense. I kept asking God for interpretation until finally, unable to have any peace about it, I painted a picture of it and showed it to two of my Bible study buddies at one of our meetings. And God gave us collectively the meaning of the vision.

The color green represents life. In this case, it meant eternal life. The pulsating shapes, like a beating heart, also represent life. The mirror images were significant with regard to redemption. In the beginning, before the fall of man, Adam and Eve were created as a mirror image (a reflection of God). When we accept the atonement and receive forgiveness for our sins through the shed blood of Jesus, we are born again. Those who are born again return to the express image of their Creator God, becoming mirror images or reflections of each other in the Spirit realm.

God used that vision of vibrant, translucent colors, pulsating shapes, and spiritual images to let me know that Hassell called upon Him in those final hours and was now in heaven, and my heavenly Father did not want me to wait until I got there to know it. Jesus said that His Holy Spirit would act as Comforter in times of sorrow (see John 14:16) as well as to empower us to be a bold witness to Him in the world (see Acts 1:8).

The power of the Holy Spirit brings God's love to His people in ways we cannot begin to fathom in our own understanding. Sometimes His love manifests in gifts of evangelism, gifts of healing, gifts of help, in prophecy, in dreams and visions, tongues, and the gift of tongues (see Joel 2:28; Acts 2:16).

A Witness

This book is a witness to that love and supernatural power. From the dreams I had as a child, to the altar at Hopewell, to the angel in my closet, to the baptism of the fire of God's Holy Spirit, to the vision of Hassell's redemption, the power of God's love wove its way into the very core of my innermost being. Shouts of joy resound within my soul as I reflect upon and testify to the manifestation of that power as my story continues.

For there is more. Much, much more.

Chapter 17

Jerusalem Arise

Holy Land Pilgrimage

After I left the Moravian church in the early 1970s, I began spending time at my brother and sister-in-law's Southern Baptist Church. I remember attending an evening service in which Jews for Jesus were featured. They were musicians, and they referred to themselves as "The Liberated Wailing Wall." I don't think my relatives will ever know how much that service impacted me. I kept their vinyl records and played them from time to time.

This was my first experience with Jewish music. Listening to their unique songs and seeing the performers wearing their Hebrew-style clothing stirred up something within me that I never felt again until a decade later when I heard Barry and Batya Segal perform and sing as worship leaders at CBU and experienced the art in worship banner presentation by Jean Mabry. These new feelings steered me toward a greater understanding of Israel's God and inspired me to learn more about my Jewish roots and how it related to my faith and lineage. I knew their God was my God, but I wanted to learn more.

A Jewish man by the name of Arthur Katz spoke at a Sunday morning worship service at Hopewell Moravian Church after Pastor Helmich died and before a new pastor was called. Impressed with his speech and in need of more practical knowledge about Christianity's Jewish roots, I bought his book, and it fed my need to go even further.

I subsequently found out that the early Moravian settlers in the area knew Hebrew and taught it to others. Nearly three decades later, I learned that the Huguenots had also taught and spoke Hebrew.

I had originally planned to go to Israel in 1998 with my Bible study leader, who was going as a volunteer with International Christian Embassy Jerusalem (ICEJ). I had my application all filled out and ready to drop into the mail, but something was wrong. Something was holding me back. Twenty-three nations founded ICEJ in 1980 in response to the U.S. and other nations not recognizing Jerusalem as the rightful place to establish their Embassy. I had been praying for discernment for weeks about how I should go. I began asking others to pray for me that I would have the wisdom to make the right decision. Finally, I completed my paperwork, got a letter of recommendation from my pastor, and was ready to drop it in the mail the next day when out of my prayer closet, I got the answer to my dilemma. The reluctance to join ICEJ had been the Holy Spirit restraining me, for God had a different plan.

Another opportunity to go that year at the same time kept appearing like a penny on my walking path. I had learned about Integrity Music's tour earlier but knew very little about the organization. I only knew that they were the music company responsible for producing Hosanna Praise and Worship CDs. I learned that Paul Wilbur was a seminar leader, singer, and songwriter with Integrity Music. Wilbur primarily writes and sings Messianic music called "Songs of Ascent" that includes any one of 15 Psalms in the series of Psalms 120 to 134. They are the same lyrics sung by Hebrew pilgrims on their way to Jerusalem or possibly while ascending Mount Zion or the steps of the Temple. They are called "Gradual Psalms," "Pilgrim Psalms," and "Psalms of Ascent." Paul has an anointed ministry whereby the Holy Spirit reaches, stirs, and opens the hearts of Christians to be reconciled to the biblical roots of their faith.

The year 1998 was important in Israel's history. The nation would not only celebrate the Feast of Tabernacles (*Sukkot*) that year, but it also marked the 50th year they would be back in their land since the Diaspora; the scattering of the Jewish people that occurred 2,000 years ago. The Feast of Tabernacles (*Sukkot*) is a God-orchestrated time to remember Israel's 40 years of wandering in the wilderness talked about in Exodus. It is also a time of celebrating the harvest. Historically, observant Jews would build a *Succah* or hut outside their homes and dwell there for a week. To some, the holiday is symbolic; they would go to hotels that have special rooms constructed for those celebrating it in a group setting, while others take it more seriously and actually live outside their own homes. I saw *Succah's* surrounded by sandbags for protection against Palestinian sniper fire, in villages such as Psagot. This Feast is the only one in which Gentiles are welcome to participate, according to Zachariah 14:16, which says that the nations will go up to Jerusalem to celebrate this Feast. Traditionally, the Jews identify this feast with the coming of the Messiah.

I called Integrity Music to learn that they would be in Jerusalem three days after Sukkot was over, not during the celebration. Their plan was to produce the "Jerusalem Arise" concert in a Jerusalem hotel at the end of the tour instead of at the beginning. I also learned that Don Moen would be repeating his "God with Us" concert in that same hotel.

It made perfect sense to mail in my application and join Susan with ICEJ, but I continued to hesitate. The importance of how I would go, who I would go with, and when I was in Jerusalem haunted me. All I really wanted was to be in the center of God's will. I wanted Him to sit down with me and say, "Judy, do it this way." So, I did the next best thing: I took it to the prayer closet.

I was at our beach house with my family but had no privacy to speak of, so I took a chair into a large, empty walk-in closet and got serious with God. I put both trips before Him as if each were on a plate. When I lifted up the ICEJ trip, there was no response. Nothing. Only silence in my spirit. But when I lifted up the Integrity Music trip, it was as if a bomb exploded in my spirit. It was a sensation that I have come to know as the quickening of the Holy Spirit.

Living water flowed from my Father's throne room straight into my heart, and I knew instantly which way I was to go. Still, like a little child, I said to God that I wanted to be in Jerusalem at the Feast of Tabernacles, and He said, "You will." Little did I know at that time what God had in mind for me.

I came out of that closet telling anyone within earshot that I knew what I was supposed to do: I was going on the Integrity Music tour. The next day, I called them to see if their itinerary had changed only to learn that they still planned to arrive in Jerusalem after, not during the Feast. Still, I signed up with Integrity, believing this was God's plan. I paid for the trip, knowing I would miss being in Jerusalem during Sukkot in the year of Jubilee. But since God had said I would be there, I figured He meant I would be there for it another year.

While I was waiting on my trip packet from Integrity Music to arrive, I continued to have peace about it. The day it came, I was in Montreat, North Carolina, with some of the women from my church sharing a house during a CBU (Christian Believers United) conference. At dinner one night, a friend said she had heard from Susan, who was already in Jerusalem preparing for ICEJ's celebration. I learned that she was about to return home to see her father one last time before his imminent passing; however, before she left the Embassy, she discovered that Paul Wilbur of Integrity Music was to be the featured artist on the last night of the Feast of Tabernacles celebration. He was set to perform and produce his "Jerusalem Arise" concert video in a live presentation at the convention center.

Did I dare believe it? Had Integrity really changed their schedule? I clutched this hope in my heart until I returned home and found my travel package from Integrity Music wedged between the storm door and the front door of my home. I held my breath as I opened the tour package and gasped when I saw that Integrity had indeed changed its itinerary. No doubt about it—we would be in Jerusalem at the beginning of the tour rather than at the end. Integrity would be producing the show at the convention center instead of at the hotel. Praise God! I would be in Jerusalem during the Feast of Tabernacles in the Year of Jubilee!

Yet, in the midst of this wonderful news, I was saddened by the fact that my friend, Susan, would not be. I attended her father's funeral, and in a bitter-sweet moment, she asked me to take a gift to one of her new friends at ICEJ. Unbeknownst to either of us, God had something unique in store for her three years later. He took her back to the land for another conference, and Susan toured the land as a pilgrim with Christian Friends of Israel, something she could not have done while at ICEJ. Glory to God, we toured together, roomed together, and worked together as volunteers at the Vision for Israel/Joseph Storehouse.

Divine Appointment and a Praise Report

As I boarded the plane to fly out of Raleigh on the Integrity Music trip to Israel, I found myself behind a flight attendant closing up the overhead compartments. Suddenly, the handle of a piece of carry-on luggage dropped down with an Integrity Music travel tag. I tapped the shoulder of the man sitting underneath it to ask if the luggage belonged to him, and he said yes. Art and his wife Jeanette were going on the same tour as me!

We had a six-hour layover in New York before our flight to Tel Aviv during which we got to know each other well. Art worked as manager of a Wal-Mart store in Raleigh. My older son, Jesse, was looking for a job. I had been praying for something out of the ordinary and asked God to provide not just any job but also one that would build his faith. I longed for it to be something my son could grab onto and see the hand of His Father in it.

Jesse had been working in Germany with the American Armed Forces Rest and Comfort unit as a ski instructor and tour guide to U.S. soldiers and their families. After getting a second degree at Appalachian State University, he worked briefly as a ski instructor at Beech Mountain, North Carolina. When I left for Israel, Jesse was recovering from a freak accident on the slopes. He broke his leg in four places; it healed, but he was now looking for a career job. After I related his story to Art, he gave me his business card and offered to help Jesse obtain a management position with Wal-Mart. After giving it some thought, Jesse accepted and pursued the opportunity.

After he finished management training, he was placed in York, South Carolina. The job quickly became a trial by fire in which my son learned endurance, perseverance, personal growth, and patience. Wal-Mart was not a good fit for a former ski instructor, mountain climber, and a totally outdoorsy kind of guy. The night shift was a nightmare for him, but God put him there for a season, and God got him out.

Jesse was only at Wal-Mart for a short time, just long enough for an associate to introduce him to his future wife. Today, they have a great marriage, and I have two wonderful granddaughters. I am so happy that God arranged this most important meeting for Jesse, and I believe that his level of faith was boosted tremendously by the experience. Glory to God.

I spent five days in Jerusalem from October 8th through the 12th. During the days leading up to the event at the convention center and the "Jerusalem Arise" concert, Don Moen and Paul Wilbur would often ride the buses with us. Chris Tomlin was also on tour, but I didn't know who he was then. I never heard of any of these famous men before the trip. When Paul performed on the last night of the International Christian Embassy's Feast of Tabernacles Celebration, an incredible anointing fell on all those in attendance. That same anointing can be still be felt when viewing the live recording of it. I am so thankful that God gave me the opportunity that night to witness what He was doing in the hearts of Christians around the world.

Angels in the Rafters

Though it was a great blessing to have been in the audience during the recording of "Jerusalem Arise," I received an even greater blessing when singer-songwriter, Don Moen, recreated his "God with Us" concert in our Jerusalem hotel. My roommate talked me into joining the choir, and the director, who used to work for Bill Gaither, pulled a great performance out of us after only one rehearsal. The night of the event, we entered into intense worship during the performance. I had never even heard of this concert before becoming part of the choir. Fortunately for me, most of the songs were traditional ones that I knew by heart. When I got back home, I made a beeline to the music store and bought the original production of Moen's concert recorded at Liberty University with Jerry Falwell, giving his personal blessing.

Near the end of the performance, the unity of our worship was so intense and the presence of the Lord so strong and mighty that I closed my eyes and let the tears stream down my cheeks. Then, suddenly, I began to hear strange voices above me, singing in a language unknown to me. I thought, Whoa! What is that? I opened my eyes and looked around only to discover that everything seemed to be normal. The next day testimonies began coming in from various people claiming to have seen (and heard) angels singing above us. It didn't seem to surprise them as much as it did me. When I was home again, I happened to be listening to a tape in which an evangelist was discussing Don Moen. He said that it was not uncommon for people to see and hear angels at his concerts. Glory to God, I was blessed to experience that!

Touring Israel

While touring Israel on this special trip, I noticed our tour guide was a bit melancholy. He was a kind Jewish man, but it was clear the historical persecution and antisemitism toward his people troubled him. Knowing that history was also weighing heavily on my mind. It broke my heart to hear him say to a busload of Christians, "I am just a Jew, a Jew-boy." I knew then I would reach out to him in some small way.

The opportunity came while he was in conversation with another tour member at the Shrine of the Book, the building that houses the Dead Sea Scrolls. She was discussing how God gave the Jewish people the Torah (Law) in order to show them their need for Jesus. I saw that he was patiently listening to her but was about to brush off her comments without receiving what she had to say. No doubt, he viewed this as just one more attempt to convert him to Christianity.

Many Christians do not realize how offensive the cross is to Jewish people because the Jews believe it was the Christians who persecuted them throughout the ages. It was at that point that I cut in and used the opportunity to share something burning in my heart just for him. I said, "I just want to thank you. I want to express my gratitude to you and your people because without the People of the Book, we wouldn't be here. Your people died to preserve what we are looking at today. The Light (word of God) has kept burning because of the Jewish people. Thank you!" In my heart, I was saying to him, "Your God is our God." He looked as if I had just poured honey over him.

I spoke up at that time because I instinctively knew in my spirit that it was inappropriate for this woman to be sharing Jesus with him no matter how true her words might have been. It is important to hear from God about the timing of truth-sharing. Otherwise, we can interfere with the Lord's preparation of hearts. And I could tell at that moment that this man would have none of it. More than once, I had seen him resist attempts by others on tour to convert him. I believe the ground (their heart) has to be softened before it can receive the rain.

The other time I connected with our guide was at the Holocaust Museum. He prepared us first with stories about the hardships his people had endured and told us that all foreign government officials are taken to the Museum because the world needed to understand why they would never give up their land. It seemed important to him that we understood as well.

As we approached the section of the tour where pictures of the children who died were suspended in mid-air while their names are read aloud, I felt such distress that I came close to hyperventilating. As we exited the building, our guide waited patiently for us to emerge and regain our composure. A few tourists were overcome with emotion, while others didn't seem affected at all. It took all my strength to stand there and listen to their responses, suppressing as much of my own emotion as I could. I heard one woman who was being comforted by a friend say, "Hitler is burning in hell," to which I mumbled that he didn't do it alone, and I noticed that our guide heard me.

Just before we entered the main part of the Museum, he had pointed to a wall sculpture entitled, "The Scream." We were about to enter the rooms that depicted the atrocities of the Holocaust when he pointed out an adjacent building telling us it was an art gallery. At that point, a woman said, "I am going to the art gallery, instead." I immediately gauged his reaction and saw the hurt in his eyes. I have always had a strong interest in art and started to follow her, but before I took another step, I asked him if the art gallery had anything to do with the Holocaust. When he said no, I wheeled around and said, "Then I am not going."

The level of respect I had just given him and his people visibly pleased him especially after he had just finished pouring his heart out to us about how important this part of the tour was to him and the Jewish people. We immediately went through the rooms that housed some of the atrocities perpetrated on his people.

Only someone who has seen "The Scream" and witnessed the account of the atrocities in the Museum can understand the depths of the horrors we encountered there. Only in Poland at the Jewish Warsaw Museum and Auschwitz did I encounter worse. Much worse.

As we exited the Museum, I told the tour guide what I had written in the journal log provided for us at the exit door. With thoughts of what he had just shared on the bus before we arrived, I wrote, "I understand." Years later, I heard Mike Huckabee share the reaction of his 11-year-old daughter, who wrote in the same book. He peeked over her shoulder to see her comment. She wrote, *"Why didn't somebody do something?"*

The Spirit of the Lord Speaks

On the flight home from this pilgrimage to the Holy Land, I ponder why God had given this trip in the way that He did. What difference did it make to God? It was then, in the quietness of the plane, that the Holy Spirit spoke to me. He showed me the response of the Gentile audience at Paul Wilbur's "Jerusalem Arise" concert. Christian hearts were united to the Hebraic aspect of their faith through the music. As I pondered this, the Spirit of the Lord said to me, "This is what I want you to see: hearts are being softened to receive what I am doing at this hour." I saw the hearts of Christians returning to their Jewish roots and the hearts of Jew and Gentile believers worshiping together as One New Man (see Ephesians 2:14-22). Christian hearts are also being softened so that they can reach out in true and unconditional love to the people of God on the other side of the cross. I saw the results first-hand. Paul Wilber himself testifies to his being born again in his Messiah Jesus Yeshua after dividing walls came down after becoming friends with an evangelical Christian. That first trip became a thread, pulling me back to the land three more times. But first, I was invited to go to China.

Chapter 18

China Outreach

Keep Your Eyes Down

When my friend from another mission trip called to tell me she was going to China and invited me to go with her, I laughed. Never having any desire to go into Asian countries and wondering what my husband would think, I said, "Boy, God would surely have to tell me to do that!" And to my amazement, He did. The moment I got serious with Him, I stopped laughing. There was a quickening in my spirit, and I knew this trip was in my immediate future. After talking to my husband, I readied myself for the mission and watched God put all the pieces together. I was about to embark on the trip of a lifetime. During a stopover in a neighboring country, we were given some unique packages to take with us into China.[72]

My check-in luggage was the very last piece of baggage to come off the plane, which meant I was the last one to leave the terminal in Beijing. While waiting for my baggage to come down the conveyor belt, I noticed a number of the contraband bags had not been picked up. I also noticed that no one was waiting for anyone else. I was all alone by the time my check-in luggage and duffel bags of contraband were piled onto my cart. I wound up with five or six extra bags because

---

[72]All names have been changed in this chapter to protect all those involved in this gigantic move of God.

some of the team members decided not to take the risk of getting through customs and had exited the terminal with the suitcases full of Bibles and tracts left on the conveyor belt.

I tried to stay close behind the last two people in our group as they went through security and exited the terminal, but I failed to keep up with them. We were told not to look at the guards or the security cameras as we exited the airport building, and with those instructions in the forefront of my mind, I had to constantly remind myself to keep calm as I maneuvered my overloaded cart through the exit doors of the airport.

By the time I got outside the terminal, every familiar face had completely disappeared. Suddenly, I realized that I was all alone with no American in sight. I paused there while I pondered what to do. I knew if I pushed my heavy cart over the metal strip in the concrete, the luggage would fall off, drawing much attention, but in the end, I had no choice. I had traveled to China with a herniated disk (later confirmed by an MRI). I could not bend over at all without extreme pain and carried a uniquely curved board in my backpack to support my back at various times when the pain was too much for me.

Finally, I gathered my strength, gave a heave, and pushed the cart forward off the sidewalk, and every piece of luggage fell off. Half of the pieces fell on one side and half on the other. Amazingly, two Chinese gentlemen jumped to my aid and stacked them all back up for me without question. Then, while I was standing there, trying to figure out where to go, a woman assigned to watch for trouble walked up and asked me if I was with a certain group of people. When I said yes, she said, "Come, I will show you where they went."

After rushing and pushing my cart across the airport parking lot, I saw volunteers from the underground churches separating the contraband from the checked luggage. My mission partner and close friend Lynette, along with all the rest of the outreach team, was already on the buses parked against the outside fence surrounding the airport. One of only two pictures taken of us at the airport that day was of me flying across the parking lot with my heavy load.

Late Night Missions

On this trip, there was an optional outreach team: volunteers who would go on a "special tour" into cities late at night, depositing hundreds of gospel tracts. They would be placing them in front of apartment buildings, buses, doorways, and window sills in China's remote areas. The rest of the team would stay behind interceding for them. I was one of 140 people selected to go on this special tour; Jenny and another traveling friend became my intercessors. I had not signed up to go originally, but when I heard the leader say they needed 50 more, I raised my hand. When I was given a paper to sign agreeing to accept the risks involved, I said, "God, if it is not Your will for me to go, You better tell me right now," and He said, "Go, I will guide you and protect you." And He did! The first night He guided me, and the second night He protected me.

The intercession was powerful, and without it, the mission would not have been such a success. The bags of contraband we carried contained 7,500 Bibles and 1 million tracts, 400,000 of which went into 37 cities in two provinces. The Bibles were given to underground churches, but the outreach teams went down dark alleyways late at night in order to take the gospel directly to the people. Reports from an underground church came back after we arrived home that a man was squatting alongside a road when small pieces of paper began fluttering from the window of a passing bus. He took the gospel tracts home, gave it to his parents, who said, "This is what we have been looking for all our lives. We knew there was a God, but we didn't know who He was or how to find Him." The parents and their son received the Lord Jesus from this one encounter with a flyer dropped out of the window of a bus. He joined the underground church and gave a glorious testimony about the obedience and sacrifice of disciples of the Lord Jesus Christ. I remember a testimony of another smuggler who was mystified to see the Bibles he had brought in being ripped apart. Aghast, he asked, "What are you doing?" to which came the response, "I got a whole chapter this time. There aren't enough to go around, so we tear the Bibles up and pass the pages out to individuals in underground churches."

Tract Trouble Ahead

I was part of Touring Team 10-B. David (not his real name) was our leader. Bob, Linda, Cindy, Letitia, and my roommate, Stella, made up the rest of the team. That first day, we traveled on a bus for 8 hours to a remote town in one of the provinces. We finally made it to our hotel late at night in the rain. I was tired and hungry. As a person with diabetes, being hungry was of concern to me, easily taken care of since all of us had snacks in our backpacks, but then a greater concern arose. We found out our hotel was an illegal hotel. People from the outside world were not supposed to be guests there. David told us if the police came to be sure to tell them how wonderful the hotel was. When we met in David's room to receive our contraband, I found a team member had taken it upon herself to smuggle into China her own American made Bible tracts to give to Chinese school children. It was the first inkling I had of the trouble that lay ahead.

We had been warned before we got to China to always do what our team leader said. We were told that the times people had been questioned and taken to the police station was when someone had his or her own agenda and would not follow their leader.

On our journeys into smaller villages, I felt like I had stepped into a time warp. Beijing is China's "show city," displaying the glory of communism, while many of the outlying towns show a different picture. Some buildings remained as they were from the time Mao took over. There were no trash cans; every day, the garbage lay on the streets until about 2:00 am when street sweepers came through to clean it up. We slept on top of our bedding and used the hot boiling water provided for tea to brush our teeth.

The commode looked like it would fall through the floor to the next level at any second. We were warned to look at the ground while walking because streets are often uneven and have gaping holes, and steps are not uniform anywhere in China. The floors in the hotel were also uneven, with multiple levels covered with carpet. On our way out that first night, I fell flat on my face, hitting my knees so hard that I had to be picked up off the floor by the other team members. David said I could go back to the room, but I answered through pain and clenched teeth, saying, "I am going!" I was not about to miss out on what God had for me to do in that city! God is not as interested in our comfort as He is in getting the job done. Fortunately, the hotel employees didn't ask to see our passport information. They just stared at us with interest and through genuine smiles. We learned later at the train station that no one in that town had ever seen Americans before. They gathered around Cindy while we were waiting, and gawked at her long blond braided hair.

David picked me to partner with him that first night, probably because he felt he needed to keep an eye on me as a diabetic. He sent us out in pairs, and because I was with him, I went further and deeper into the streets and alleys than the other team members did. I learned a lot from watching David that night. Once, he saved me from stepping into a huge, gaping hole by yanking me across it before I even realized it was there.

Around 1:30 am, David and I went into a courtyard, and he left me there in the lighted enclosure while he went down an extremely dark side street. It seemed as if he had stepped off the Earth's face when he disappeared into the thick darkness. While I waited, I looked around for a place to lay my tracts. To my right was an apartment building. On the opposite side of the expanse was a loading dock in front of a warehouse.

I immediately made my way to the apartment building, happy to be able to lay down multiple sets of tracts. My goal was to give out all the tracts, and apartment buildings were great places to do that. I could put down ten booklets (instead of just one) at apartment buildings. David had instructed me to either toss the tracts onto the bottom set of steps from a distance or go under the first set of steps and place them closer to the doorway. To get to the doorway in the stairwell, one had to bend over and go under the first set of steps, but in doing so, it would put me more at risk of getting caught. Still, I chose the latter because it guaranteed that the tracts would be found.

However, the moment the tracts left my hand and hit the concrete, light flooded the stairwell, and at the same time, I heard the roaring of an engine and saw the lights of a vehicle approaching. My American brain screamed, POLICE! I really believed I was in trouble, but I kept my head and quickly looked around, trying to decide what to do. If discovered, it might mean being taken to the police station for questioning, and perhaps even deportation since the tracts I had just placed was a witness against me. I felt I would be trapped in just a few moments.

I frantically looked around for a place to hide as I made my way into the middle of the courtyard. To my right, I saw that a section of the wall opposite the entrance to the courtyard was recessed, creating a shadow. I headed for it and had just enough time to step into it when the vehicle came roaring into the courtyard. To my relief, it was not the police but a huge service truck.

The driver pulled up and parked at the loading dock right in front of me! The driver side of the truck was opposite where I was, but I knew I was not out of trouble. I knew the man would get out and see me standing there in the shadow as he made his way back across the courtyard to the apartment building! I had one second to do something. A woman hiding in a dark corner of a courtyard in the wee hours of the morning would have a tough time explaining why she was there, especially if she were an American, did not speak Chinese, and was found in a forbidden city. I knew I had to move!

I stepped out and away from the wall, forcing myself to walk slowly toward the center of the enclosure. I was wearing my Gore-Tex all-weather coat and a ball cap David had given me. I thought that if I got my back to him, he could not tell that I was a woman. It worked. I never looked back. I could tell the man was right behind me as we both walked away from the truck. He coughed, and I could feel his breath only inches away. He was headed for the apartment building with all those tracts, and I was headed out of the courtyard. I made it out of the enclosure and waited for David.

In a few moments, I heard footsteps. Was it the truck driver or my partner? I was unnerved but not paralyzed with fear; I knew God had me. Within moments, my partner stepped out of the shadows. I never told him what had just happened, and we walked slowly and silently back to our lodging for the night.

The next day we found there was no bus connection to our next destination, so we traveled by train to another city hoping to find a place to leave tracts. This particular city was a huge metropolitan area. All the other outreach teams were flying there the next day for the final flight back to Beijing.

David did not want to leave tracts there because it was a much more dangerous city with tighter security. We began searching for a place to stay in a more remote section of the city, hoping to find a safer place to tract. After deciding it was not safe, we headed back to the city's main hub. When we finally found a hotel, it was on the corner of a busy four-lane intersection. Our passports were scrutinized to the fullest. If we got caught, we would be connected to the ministry team coming into the city the next day. Even so, a member of our team insisted we tract there, and finally the decision was made—we would do it.

Cindy, Oh Cindy!

Cindy, an accomplished world traveler who had brought her brand of tracts along, had her own agenda. She began usurping authority over our leader at every turn, attempting to make decisions affecting the safety of the entire team and the larger mission endeavor as a whole. Dissension and disunity quickly surfaced among us.

I want to inject here that Satan uses the weakness of our flesh to weaken and destroy our goals while accomplishing his own. Here, he distracted and misled a dear woman of God whose heart for children, coupled with arrogance and self-motivation, led her to act against the will of her Father and our mission outreach.

No matter how sincere one thinks their motives are, the devil and his minions will use those motives against them if he can. The fruit of this event changed all of us, especially the woman causing the problem. I bumped into her on my next mission trip and found her to be a totally different person, full of patience, kindness, and grace. Cindy and I became drama team partners in another country.

But here? I give absolute praise and honor to God the Father and the Holy Spirit for what happened in those next few hours in Wuhan. When we met in David's room to pray and finalize our plans for the night, the level of discord grew so high that Stella refused to go out into the streets of the city until we talked about it. She turned to the team member causing the confusion and confronted her. She said we were grieving the Holy Spirit, and she would not go out on such a dangerous mission without His anointing and protection.

David recognized what was happening and immediately addressed the real issue. He told us that there was a war going on in the atmosphere above us because someone was going to get saved that night, and the battle was manifesting itself in us! He advised us not to say another word about the problem but to pray against bad attitudes.

What happened next is one of the highlights of my life. There was repentance. There was a confession. There was a submission to the Holy Spirit like I had never seen before. Individual egos were put on the altar and submitted to our Lord. After repentance, there was intercession and warfare led by the Holy Spirit. I remember praying in the language of the Spirit (out loud) with such force that it surprised me. My roommate and I both found ourselves interceding in a language with words that felt and sounded like bullets rising up from deep within and hitting an unseen target. Inexplicable, except to say the words were living waters flowing from that all-consuming fire from the Holy Spirit for a specific purpose. It reminded me of 1 Corinthians 12:4-11.

> *Now there are distinctive varieties and distributions of endowments (gifts, extraordinary powers distinguishing certain Christians, due to the power of divine grace operating in their souls by the Holy Spirit), and they vary, but the [Holy] Spirit remains the same. And there are distinctive varieties of service and ministration, but it is the same Lord [Who is served]. And there are distinctive varieties of operation [of working to accomplish things], but it is the same God Who inspires and energizes them all in all.] But to each one is given the manifestation of the [Holy] Spirit [the evidence, the spiritual illumination of the Spirit] for good and profit.] To one is given in and through the [Holy] Spirit [the power to speak] a message of wisdom, and to another [the power to express] a word of knowledge and understanding according to the same [Holy] Spirit; To another [wonder-working] faith by the same [Holy] Spirit, to another the extraordinary powers of healing by the one Spirit;] To another the working of miracles, to another prophetic insight (the gift of interpreting the divine will and purpose); to another the ability to discern and distinguish between [the utterances of true] spirits [and false ones], to another various kinds of [unknown] tongues, to another the ability to interpret [such] tongues.]*

All these [gifts, achievements, abilities] inspired and brought to pass by one and the same [Holy] Spirit, Who apportions to each person individually [exactly] as He chooses (AMP).

In China, it became imperative that the gifting of the Spirit be in operation and utilized as the Spirit gave them utterance, so we submitted ourselves to the anointing. We all knew when the enemy fled. There was a tremendous feeling of release and peace as the Spirit of God flooded the room. It was physical, and we immediately began to worship!

However, Cindy, who had been challenging David's leadership at every turn, missed out on the power of this Holy Spirit prayer time. She did not participate in any of it. She left the room, saying she did not need any more prayer because her friends back home were praying.

Thank God she came back. For all we knew she had gone out on the streets by herself trying to lay down all those tracts that clearly showed an American company made them with Chinese translation. When she returned, we were in a circle singing and hugging one another. We asked if we could pray for her, and this time she relented, saying, "Sure, go for it!" I recall being pleased that she put her arm around me (and pinched my back). I was thankful I had been kind to her during the confrontation. We went out on the streets that night with unity flowing, confident in the power and protection of the Holy Spirit. That night I was partnered with Bob and perhaps because I had been with our leader, David, the night before, I ventured further down darker alleyways than my partner wanted to go. I was totally focused and determined to go back to the hotel with all my assigned tracts left on the streets.

The Stranger

My next experience would not have happened if the Holy Spirit had not restrained us in that hotel room. It also would not have happened if we had not had the corporate prayers of the rest of the mission team like my friends who had remained behind joining the team of intercessors.

David taught me to tract on the way out of an alley or street instead of on the way in. He advised me to look at the end of the streets and skip it if there was a light coming from a side street. Bob and I were getting increasingly uneasy due to the high volume of traffic on these city streets. After discovering that others had already laid down tracts ahead of us, we decided it best to head back toward our hotel. However, to leave the immediate area, we had to pass through a wide brick-lined thoroughfare just off the main street.

Suddenly, I discovered a street that looked empty of people and empty of tracts. The intense desire to leave all my tracts on the streets that night overwhelmed me. Returning to our hotel with empty pockets was my goal for more than one reason. Prior to the trip, mission members were asked to take only one piece of check-in luggage. The reason for it could not be divulged, so instead of obeying in blind faith, some called the airline, found out they could take two, and so they did. Remembering the look on the faces of our mission leaders when they discovered hundreds of Bibles and tracts would not reach lost souls in China due to the extra pieces of luggage made me even more determined to discharge all the tracts assigned to Bob and me.

On the other side of this thoroughfare, people were milling around and eating from gas grills most likely set up by the government. Apartment complexes lined the street I was on, and I saw a chance to put down the rest of my tracts. I was so intent on my mission that I did not notice the lights flooding into the end of this street from an adjoining side street. I saw no one and heard no one. The street was empty when I ventured down it while Bob waited for me at its entrance.

Halfway down the street, I turned to look at the doorway of an apartment complex. I fixed my mind on where I would leave my tracts on the way out, but when I turned back around to face the end of the street again, a man was standing squarely in front of me, blocking my path. I nearly bumped into him. I did not look up at his face, but I did get an impression of his overall appearance. He was dressed all in black, and I think there was a hood on his head. I am 5'5" and my head came to the lower half of his chest, just above the waist. He seemed to be in a military stance with his arms and hands hanging down by his side. Falling back upon the advice we were given, if we got caught, I yelled up the street, "Bob, I think I got lost again." Then I wheeled around and slowly began making my way back up the street toward my partner. The hair on the back of my neck stood up. I expected a hand to clamp down on my shoulder at any moment, but none came. There was only silence. I expected the man to follow me, but I heard no footsteps behind or going down the street from whence he came. None. The man just vanished. I did not think any more about it until my head hit the pillow that night.

As soon as I closed my eyes, I saw that same street again clear as crystal but without the man in it. Then God began showing me why this was no ordinary occurrence. The man I bumped into was no ordinary Chinese. He let me figure it out as more and more revelation came. The clincher came the moment God showed me that, unlike the previous night, I was not afraid, though, in reality, I was in much more danger. I began to see and understand what it was that my Father was trying to tell me. The man was not in my vision because he was not a man; he was my guardian angel.

It has been said that angels sent from God arrive, get the job done, and leave. They do not hang around drawing attention to themselves. As I received this revelation, I got so excited I wanted to get up and run about. I wanted to tell others, but I waited until the next morning.

Gradually, the memory of the encounter began to impact me in a unique way. I felt an extraordinary intimacy with the memory of my connection to the unknown stranger. For many days, even on the plane ride home, I continued to feel a warm, loving embrace whenever I thought about it. It was not the first time I had come into contact with an angel, so it wasn't hard for me to receive and believe what God had shown me.

The next morning, I learned that Cindy, the woman with her own agenda and tracts, was mugged in front of a Buddhist Temple. She had been looking for a school to drop off all those tracts she had brought specifically for children. Out of a group of Chinese men, one had grabbed her satchel containing all of her American made tracts and her passport! We were told that passports sell for $5,000 each on the black market.

When the man grabbed for it, she yanked it back, falling to the ground, and somehow retaining her bag. I asked her partner, "What did you do?" Leticia, a short Latino woman, said she held up her umbrella in a threatening position, and they all took off running. After relating what had happened to me, I said, "Don't you think they might have seen someone behind you that caused them to flee?" And she agreed.

What an awesome God we serve! He protected those women, and He protected me. But more importantly, He protected His Word. After the mission ended, David (my outreach partner) went into closed Provinces at great risk to continue what we had started. As a result of a seven-year endeavor, all the cities in China have been covered with the word of God. I saw its fruit when I returned twelve years later with my sister, her son, and daughter-in-law to adopt a Chinese baby boy. Shop owners were talking freely about Jesus. One openly displayed his Bible on the countertop. Though times have changed, I was told that discretion and caution are still advised regarding Christian evangelism. The Chinese government routinely rounds up Christians in home churches to persecute or imprison them. As an extra precaution during our outreach in China, we always had our meetings in a hotel other than the one we were staying in. Also, my outreach partner, Stella, was not my regular roommate.

The night before we flew home from our special tour, we had the privilege of meeting the leader of China's underground church. He had come to speak at our celebration dinner but opted to have an interpreter speak for him. This man was imprisoned when Mao came to power simply because he was a Christian. He related some of the tortures used against him, saying he could stop the torture by saying three words: "I don't believe." But he never did. I noticed that much caution was taken to keep prying eyes out of our private dining room that evening. He was whisked in and out of the banquet room through a side door without anyone from the hotel staff seeing him.

Connecting the Dots

Jesus said, "But you shall receive power (ability, efficiency, and might) when the Holy Spirit has come upon you, and you shall be my witnesses in Jerusalem and all Judea and Samaria and to the ends (the very bounds) of the earth" (Acts 1:8 AMP)

China was one of the places that the living waters of the Holy Spirit poured forth from my innermost being in ways I had never encountered before. Jesus said that we would receive dunamis (power) after the Holy Spirit came upon us—the power to witness and power to take the gospel to the far side of the earth. I walked in that power at the airport, in the courtyard, on the streets, in the hotel room, and in the unity that brought Holy Spirit anointing for protection when danger lurked in places we could not anticipate or prevent.

In China, I knew what it was to walk in the center of God's will for me. Living waters flowed to equip the saints to carry out the mission successfully. Glory to God! The China outreach was one of the highlights of my life.

Chapter 19

The Seed Pearl

After my amazing trip to China, I received an invitation to travel to two Islamic countries. Kazakhstan was one of them, and the other was so tightly closed to the gospel that it is too dangerous to speak its name. This beautiful, mysterious, Arab country opened its doors to Christian tour groups for a brief period in 2000. God opened this door for me while I was still in China. God beckoned, and I responded with a yes in my heart even while I was struggling to believe my Father meant for me to go. I am so thankful that He sufficiently raised my faith level and confidence for me to make such a trip. I knew traveling to a Muslim region of the world would be an extraordinary challenge and adventure for me. I asked God to send someone to accompany me, and to my amazement, He provided a former roommate from a previous mission trip. She had always had a heart for Muslims, and this trip was very special for her.

Arabic Tapes

A week or two before we were to depart, a church member cleaned out her garage and found the entire Bible on cassette tapes in Arabic. Her father was from one of the countries we were about to visit, and the tapes were his. At our church commissioning service the night before we were to go, she came up to me and asked if I would take the Bible on cassette tapes. I didn't have the heart to tell her that my leaders in New York might confiscate them because it was too dangerous for the mission members to have them in their possession, but I agreed to take them out of compassion for her enthusiasm and zeal.

The following day, my husband and I swung by her house to pick them up on the way to the airport. My bags were so full I had to put them in the outside zippered pocket of my roommate's bag. When we got to New York, I told the director about the tapes thinking she would tell me to throw them away. Instead, she waved me on and said, "We will decide about that later."

However, no decision was ever made, and we arrived around 2:00 am with no one in the terminal except our group. Customs did not inspect our luggage, but to my surprise and horror, my roommate put her luggage on the counter for inspection. I thought my heart would stop, but they waved her through without looking in her luggage.

We were informed that the level of freedom in this country was very limited and, in some parts, nonexistent. It is a criminal offense for anyone to bring in more than one Bible. Christians are allowed to own a Bible in English, but it is forbidden to own one in Arabic under penalty of deportation, imprisonment, or death. And, no one can evangelize Arab citizens under penalty of death. I was told that Arab men in this particular place view women as nothing more than dogs and that they can do with foreign women as they please. While we were there, a woman from Switzerland went out alone and was never heard from again.

I remember we were in one of our rooms praying early one morning and were getting a little exuberant in our worship. A moment later, our leader rapped on the door and said, "Ladies, you cannot do that here." We were reminded that we had to watch ourselves when worshiping or praying unless we were at the only compound available to us located in a little square where foreign workers are allowed to practice their religion. No foreigner can go outside that restricted courtyard to share the gospel for any reason.

That first night in this darkest of regions, I carried my precious cargo, the Bible on tape in Arabic, with me to our first service. I began to ask the Lord what I was to do with the tapes realizing that I was walking in blind faith. Who was I supposed to give them to?

The Seed Pearl

Should I present them to the minister in charge of the service or someone else? I looked across the aisle and saw a woman (whom I later learned was a worker from a neighboring country). I heard the Holy Spirit say, "She is the one. Give them to her."

But I did not dare to exercise my faith enough to do it. I did not know if she even spoke English. Was I hearing correctly? I felt the pressure build inside me as the service ended. By the time we exited the building, I was greatly distressed that I had not approached her. My indecisiveness kept me from reaching out in faith to this woman. I had not been obedient and was devastated that I had missed my chance. I began praying for God to give me another opportunity. Fear had entered my heart, fear that the tapes would not be respected, even wasted, if given to the wrong person. Hence, fear had replaced obedience and faith.

The next night, we arrived a little early, and I saw the same lady sitting about four rows in front of me in the same spot as she was before. She was sitting by herself, and there was an empty seat beside her. After my failure the previous night, I was determined to carry out my mission no matter what. This night, I was more willing than confident as I went over and sat down. Her English was limited, but we could communicate. I shared with her as best as I could that I had the Bible on cassette tapes in Arabic and that the Lord wanted me to give the tapes to her. That is when she revealed to me she was a lay minister and was associated with the group we were visiting. She took the tapes from me and said, "I have to go because I am a greeter."

I noticed that she left her pocketbook in her chair beside me (a total stranger) but took the tapes, clutching them to her as she greeted those coming in. When I saw her at the end of the night, she pointed to heaven and said, "We will see each other again."

I stepped out in faith with that particular woman, trusting God's choice to leave the tapes with her. I soon realized that had I given the tapes to the assemblies' pastors, they might have misused them or destroyed them in fear. I knew those cassette tapes would be copied and used as the Lord guided and that sharing the Bible in this form would make for a wider distribution than would one single Arabic Bible.

The Vision

During our first nightly service in this spiritually darkest of countries, I had a strange vision. I saw what looked like four seeds against a black background. When I asked the Lord what it was, I received the word "seed." But there were four. It was much later that I understood the significance of the number four.

The next morning during our private worship time, the vision came again. This time there was only one seed, but I heard two words, "seed pearl." Aha! I had an idea what a seed pearl was, but I had to wait until I got home to confirm it. On the way home from the airport, I quizzed my husband about the seed pearl, and he briefly explained it to me, and it was just as I thought. Soon I made a trip to the library to learn more, and it was then that I got excited.

I remember reading about how cultivators grow pearls in a cultured oyster bed. Submerged in total darkness, they take the oysters out at night and pry them open. Then they place an irritant like a seed such as a piece of shell or sand inside them. The irritant or seed is put there to inflame the oyster and cause it to secrete a substance that hardens over it. As this substance grows larger, it causes the oyster to make a pearl.

Interestingly, the part of the oyster covering the seed pearl during formation is referred to as a "mantle," like the mantle spoken of in the Bible. Biblically speaking, we find the mantle or cloak served the practical purpose of keeping people warm and protecting them from the elements. It also serves a symbolic purpose, as in the case of the prophets showing they were wrapped in God's authority. Like all imagery in the Old Testament, the mantle presents a visible representation of a New Testament principle. The mantle can be seen as a symbol of the anointing of the Holy Spirit Whom God so graciously gives to all Christians, the people of His choosing (see 1 Thessalonians 1:5-6; 1 Peter 2:9).[73]

---

[73] Logos (n.d.). GotQuestions.org, "What is a mantle in the Bible?" Retrieved from http://www.gotquestions.org/mantle-Bible.html.

The Seed Pearl

Farmers have to leave the oysters alone for three years for the best chance of cultivating a pearl. After that, they pry the oysters open, hoping to find a valuable pearl inside. I discovered that the first pearls ever to be discovered and mined were in that same Arab region of the world where the vision occurred.[74]

The vision of the seed pearl referred to the tapes I had brought with me and left in that dark country that was closed to the gospel. Just like those oysters in a cultured bed, there is no guarantee that a pearl will develop from the irritant placed inside. Persons in other countries who are persecuted for their faith but cleave to that faith anyway are like an oyster that grows a beautiful pearl. They receive strength and the ability to see a result because of their trials. Thus, the seed pearl (the abrasive foreign substance) inserted into an oyster for purposes of producing a cultured pearl under controlled conditions is a metaphor regarding God's purposes in spiritually dark places. We are the seed pearls depositing the light of the gospel in such countries.

The light of the gospel, no matter how abrasive it might be, will eventually produce a pearl of great price: Jesus manifesting in the lives of those walking in darkness. The mollusks are picked up in darkness, pried open to insert the seed pearl, put back in the water, and left alone in total darkness for a time to either produce fruit or not. To me, the four seeds represented the four people in leadership for this missionary effort; the single seed represented the gospel in the Arabic language.

---

[74] Ibid.

Chapter 20

Drama Team

Bolivia and Quito, Ecuador

Soon, I had an opportunity to participate in another mission outreach with some of my former mission partners, but, unlike them, I became part of the drama team performing on the streets in Quito, Ecuador, and at La Paz Stadium, Bolivia. The entire outreach team passed out tracks on the streets of Quito, mountaintop communities, and various places in Bolivia.

We prayed for people to be healed of diseases, conducted street deliverances, and led many to the Lord through an interpreter. I saw blind eyes healed and people getting out of wheelchairs. One person I prayed for had a growth disappear from her neck. One of her eyes was also misaligned, and after prayer, her vision was restored, and her eye came back into proper position on her face: a visual manifestation of the healing power of God.

One afternoon in Quito, Ecuador, as I was handing out flyers inviting people to come to our nightly meetings, I came upon a demon-possessed woman writhing on the ground. Seeing some of my teammates attempting to cast the demons out, I walked up and joined in. The woman had many demons that were not easily leaving. She had thrown up mucus-like fluid, which is common when demons depart a host body. During this deliverance process, I happened to drop the flyers, and they touched the edge of the liquid. When I reached down and picked them up, a momentary weakness surged through my body. Beginning in my feet, it raced up my legs, through my body, and out the top of my head. This sensation traveled through me like lightning and left me feeling faint. Needless to say, it gave me cause for alarm.

Later that evening, during dinner, I told my teammates what had happened because I was concerned that there had been a transfer of some sort and that a demon had latched onto me. They made light of it and said it was impossible because we were covered with the blood of Jesus. Once home, though, it continued to bother me, and I thought about counseling. I came close to asking an elder of my church about it.

Finally, I received an understanding. Discernment. The Lord spoke to me about what happened that day. He said that it was not a demon I had received but an experience that He allowed me to have in order to teach me a lesson. He wanted me to experience the weakness of the flesh when one tries to minister in such a situation without the unction, direction, or protection of the Holy Spirit. I should not have participated in that situation because I had not been called to do so by the Holy Spirit. I received this as the truth because I had peace thereafter.

And this valuable lesson proved invaluable in my future ministry. I never again interfered directly with the demonic unless specifically called to by God, nor did I speak directly into that realm of darkness unless under the power, direction, and guidance of the Holy Spirit.

CHAPTER 21

TWO MISSION TRIPS TO THE LAND

One night, in the spring of 2001, a former mission partner of mine walked into our For Zion's Sake meeting, waving a brochure from Christian Friends of Israel. She was suggesting that we go on this trip to visit the land of Israel, which included a conference and tour of special sites with David Dolan, former CBS news correspondent, international speaker, and author. The conference was to be held in Jerusalem during Shavuot. Shavuot is one of the Lord's feasts and a special time of celebration for Christians since it was during Shavuot (Pentecost) that the Holy Spirit of fire fell on the disciples in the upper room. Pentecost is Greek for the Hebrew word Shavuot, also called the Feasts of Weeks, for it comes 50 days after Passover. For us Christians, it is 50 days after the death and resurrection of Jesus Christ. Shavuot or Pentecost is important for it marks the date of the birthing of the Christian Church (see Acts 2).

After she left, I said to Debbie, co-leader of For Zion's Sake (FZS), "I think I am supposed to go on this trip." She responded by saying, "I think we are all supposed to go," meaning all FZS members. On the way home, I turned to the Lord and pondered all that had transpired that night. At first, I thought God was issuing a personal invitation for me to go, not realizing at the time that He meant for all of us to go.

After I got home, I lay in bed, wondering how I was going to tell my husband that God was calling me to go back to Israel. After all, I had been once as a pilgrim in 1998. This time I would be attending the Shavuot conference in Jerusalem, followed by a tour with David Dolan and CFI. We would visit locations not covered on the Integrity Music tour of 1998. It was then that the Lord dropped a bombshell. I began to think about remaining in Israel for an additional week for volunteer work at The Joseph Storehouse.

Glory to God. My husband consented, and before I knew it, the rest of my FZS group and I went for the conference and tour, followed by volunteer work. My son, John, went with us as a first-time pilgrim.

The Joseph Storehouse

We left Jerusalem after the Shavuot conference early Sunday morning on May 24, 2001. I was walking through Hezekiah's tunnel when a bomb detonated on Ben Y'huda Street. Some of us had been on that same street the day before. We learned that the perpetrator could not get his van parked close enough to do the intended damage, so no one was seriously injured.

Because our tour group was small (only 13 of us), our time spent touring with David Dolan was unique. We had one-on-one time with him. We picked up David after we left Hezekiah's tunnel and spent the week traveling to places that were not open to most groups.

I swam in the Sea of Galilee and visited a cave on the side of a hill, believed by some to be the actual site of the Mount of Beatitudes (where Jesus gave His famous speech). This alternate location fits the biblical description perfectly while the other is actually too high and too distant for His followers to have heard him even if one takes into account terrain changes through 2,000 years.

We traveled to the Golan Heights, visiting Nimrod's Castle and Caesarea Philippi. We also visited the northern perimeter of Israel's border with Syria and Lebanon.

At Kibbutz Malkia, an Israeli commune bordering Lebanon, we spoke with Eitan, a farmer with an apple orchard that faces South Lebanon. The Hezbollah militia often lay in wait there for

Two Mission Trips to the Land

an opportunity to shoot down on anyone passing through. The Hezbollah is a part of the Syrian army and is usually stationed along the southern Lebanon border.

Eitan spoke with us at great length. He carried us into the bomb shelter in the center of the kibbutz showing us places tourists don't normally see. We visited the nearby military base on the Israeli-Lebanon border. We spoke to Yoni, a young soldier originally from England. We were not allowed to take pictures within the base itself, but Yoni allowed us to photograph a tank returning from patrol. We learned they were on high alert that day due to the one-year anniversary of Israel Defense Forces' (IDF) pullout from South Lebanon. Fortunately, there was no trouble that day.

We had a sweeping, panoramic view of the landscape due to the height of that outpost. We could see the new road being built so that the children from Kibbutz Malkia would not have to ride their school bus on the dangerous road along the Lebanon border. We were told that at that very moment, the Hezbollah militia had us in their gun-sights.

From the Kibbutz Malkia, we went to Safed, which is another Jewish community close to the border. That morning we received news that a suicide bomber murdered 19 Russian immigrants in a Tel Aviv club the night before. Because of that, our farewell dinner in Old Jaffa was canceled because authorities feared an organized protest from Israeli citizens demanding retaliation. Tel Aviv is the modern-day Jaffa.

We went to Old Jaffa to see Paul's house, where Peter had his vision concerning God's desire to take the Gospel to the Gentiles. Old Jaffa was empty of tourists and residents on the streets that afternoon due to barricades by Israeli police preventing access to the Arab neighborhoods (to protect its Arab citizens from harm). The following day, my son and a few other members of the tour group returned to the U.S. while the six friends from the FZS group, Susan, Debbie H., Debbie C., Cheryl, Gloria, Jean, and I remained behind to do volunteer work at The Joseph Storehouse in Abu Gosh or Christian Friends of Israel headquarters in Jerusalem. I stayed in Abu Gosh at a French convent bed and breakfast run by the Sisters of St. Joseph's.

Sister Catherine, a nun from this French order, visits Bethlehem once a week to help the Arab-Christians living there. Terrorist groups set up military bases in many of their business establishments to fire upon the Israeli citizens whenever possible. When the IDF finds them in Arab Christian businesses, they destroy them to protect the Israeli citizens. Unfortunately, this results in the destruction of the Arab-Christian businesses and their means to make a living as well. In 1998, our Israeli tour guide stopped at several Arab shops in order for us to buy souvenirs from the local Arab businessmen. We also ate at an Arab restaurant in order to support their business. But in 2001, no tourist was allowed into Bethlehem much less frequent the Arab shops. The Christian Arabs did not get the tourist trade, and near-famine conditions forced citizens to beg on the streets. After any Arab bombing attack, the IDF closes the border, making living conditions even worse for the peaceful inhabitants.

The citizens of Abu Gosh comprise a community of Arabs who love Israel and even fought beside them in the 1948 war. They had thriving businesses, nice homes, and good roads. Tradition holds that the Ark of the Covenant sat at Abu Gosh for a time before King David brought it back into Jerusalem.

2001 | Vision for Israel - Joseph Storehouse
Malachi (staff), Judy, Debbie, Susan, Gloria Jean

Two Mission Trips to the Land

I spent five days working at The Joseph Storehouse, vacuuming floors, cleaning windows, dusting, and organizing shelves. I remember cleaning under Barry Segal's desk while he was sitting at it! Gloria Jean and I rearranged the items in the tiny shop for display purposes. Though we transferred, organized, labeled, and inventoried their supplies when we got in their way we felt Barry and Batya were the ones blessing us instead of the other way around.

2001 | Judy volunteering at The Joseph Storehouse

My favorite memory was the early morning prayer time spent with The Joseph Storehouse staff and other volunteers. Malachi, a Storehouse staff member, picked us up and returned us to the convent each day to save us from the long walk through the Arab neighborhood of Abu Gosh. Abu Gosh purportedly was a safe neighborhood, but we were spared the long trek back and forth through it to the convent. Malachi saw to it that we were never idle. At the end of the week, we left with a wonderful sense of a job well done, a precious new family of believing friends, and a lot of sore muscles.

Two events stand out in my mind as I think back on my time as a volunteer there. One morning, Barry arrived while we were having our early morning prayers. He was visibly upset because an Arab businessman from Bethlehem had been murdered. The man had pleaded for a bulletproof vest, but Barry could not get one to him until after the weekend, and by that time, it was too late. In Bethlehem, members of the Fatah, Arafat's terrorist organization, had threatened to kill him if he did not join them. These vests range in cost from two to three thousand dollars, and the Storehouse could only afford to buy them through financial donations. Fortunately, my other memory is less tragic. On the morning we were scheduled to leave, my friends and I gathered on the bluff behind the French Order's Convent for a special time of worship and prayer. This mountaintop retreat seemed close to paradise to us with its serenity, cool breezes, and gorgeous blooming plants. Sister Catherine was truly a sister in the Lord. She and The Joseph Storehouse team work closely together to supply the needs of the Arabs and the Jews. Barry and Batya have been known to use the convent grounds for VFI's special services.

A predominately Christian Arab village, Abu Gosh was built over the ruins of the biblical town of Kiryat Ye'arim (meaning town of forests), which is identified in Joshua 9:17 as the ritual center where the Ark of the Covenant was placed after it was returned from the country of the Philistines (see 1 Samuel 6:6-12). During the Byzantine period, Kiryat Ye'arim was sanctified because of its traditional connection to the Ark of the Covenant, and a church was built there. It remains to this day within the confines of the French Order.

2001 | Susan waving flag over Abu Gosh with Jerusalem in the background

Shout to the North and South

This beautiful spot overlooks the town with Jerusalem in the distance. Susan and I waved our flags high in the air to Robin Marks' song, "Shout to the North and South, Shout to the East and West; that Jesus Christ is Lord of all."[75]

Our hearts were filled with joy as we waved our flags over this beautiful, and tormented nation. I was struck with a keen sense of love and sympathy for all the people of this land, both peace-loving ones and angry-hate filled ones, because I knew they all had one thing in common—they all needed the love of the Jewish Messiah (Yeshua/Jesus). They all needed to know the Father of the Universe who had created them for fellowship, communion, and relationship. I will forever cherish those final moments in the land, and this trip as one of the highlights of my life. I didn't know it then, but I would soon be returning to the land that I came to love and the people I cared for so deeply.

Returning to the land five months later might be viewed by some as unusual, even excessive, but in God's timeframe, it was not. He beckoned, and I followed.

And I am so thankful He did. For unbeknownst to me, the *Mission of Solidarity* held an important divine appointment having far-reaching consequences. And so it was that I went once again to Israel, with CFI in the fall of 2001.

Mission of Solidarity

Comfort ye, comfort ye My people, says your God (Isaiah 40 AMP)

To grant [consolation and joy] to those who mourn in Zion—to give them an ornament (a garland or diadem) of beauty instead of ashes, the oil of joy instead of mourning, the garment [expressive] of praise instead of a heavy, burdened, and failing spirit—that they may be called oaks of righteousness [lofty, strong, and magnificent, distinguished for uprightness, justice, and right standing with

---

[75] Listen to "Revival in Belfast" at "Shout to the North" by Robin Marks at www.youtube.com/watch?v=4ERrNP187qo.

God], the planting of the Lord, that He may be glorified. And they shall rebuild the ancient ruins; they shall raise up the former desolations and renew the ruined cities, the devastations of many generations. (Isaiah 61:2-4 AMP)

For Zion's sake will I not hold my peace, and for Jerusalem's sake I will not rest until her imputed righteousness and vindication go forth as brightness, and her salvation radiates as does a burning torch. (Isaiah 62:1 AMP)

You [Judah] shall no more be termed Forsaken, nor shall your land be called Desolate any more. But you shall be called Hephzibah [My delight is in her], and your land be called Beulah [married]; for the Lord delights in you, and your land shall be married [owned and protected by the Lord.] (Isaiah 62:4 AMP)

I flew out of the States on September 29th, just weeks after 9/11. Signing up late, I took the only flight available, which was French air. France subsidizes their flights, so I was able to go when other airlines either canceled or condensed flights. The purpose of this mission was to connect with and show solidarity with those "people of the book," that is, the Jews who believe in God's covenant promises to them as descendants of Abraham, Isaac, and Jacob about the land. Specifically, they are people dwelling in the communities of Judea and Samaria. Our mission to the unbelieving Jewish community was simply to be ambassadors of faith, love, and reconciliation to them and to remove the "stones of stumbling" put there by the church's long years of persecution. Thank God the door is now open for dialogue as it has never been before.

The Mission of Solidarity Team consisted of Canadians and South Africans, along with people from the United Kingdom, Slovakia, and the United States. There were two brothers from the former Czechoslovakia who shared their ministry outreach to Holocaust Survivors in Poland.

Five years later, I came face to face with the impact these two brothers would have on my life. I find it hard to express the depth of which is so profound and life-changing without weeping its remembrance.

Two Mission Trips to the Land

Roman and Stanislaw Gawel, whom I call the Gawel brothers, always sat at the back of our bulletproof bus when we went into the disputed territories. One day when I was returning to my seat after having played a special song over the speakers, one of them met me in the aisle and asked if I would send him a copy of it. I responded by simply giving him the cassette tape as a gift.

The Hebrew song, Sh'ma Elohai, had no English translation, but the emotion it generates is tangible. Without having to know the meaning, the heart cries along with the sound of it. I imagine the Gawel brothers understood it, but it was years before I obtained the translation. The song is a cry to God to stop the pain and suffering of His people. I will always remember these lyrics, "The heart sinks down, and one cannot bear it any longer." But on that day in 2001, since most of us did not know Hebrew, I asked everyone to please listen with their hearts. When one of the Gawel brothers asked for a copy, I was blessed to know that the song meant so much to him.

The night before our mission began, we met for a prayer convocation on Jerusalem's southern steps. We were just finishing up and begin to praise and worship the Lord when the recorded chant from the Al-Aqsa Mosque directly above us began its call to worship. This chant is played over a loudspeaker, so Muslims in the immediate area of Jerusalem hear it and respond. Our response was spontaneous and loud.

We began shouting "hallelujahs" and praises to God. It was incredible to suddenly hear the voices of 300-400 Christians shouting at the top of their lungs and effectively drowning out the sound coming from the mosque above us. Once the call to worship ended, we broke into music and song.

I was so proud to be part of this call to worship. I also was aware that a group of Orthodox Jews on their way to the Western Wall for evening prayers had paused to watch us. I wondered what they were thinking. I found out a few days later when one of them, a representative of Beit Daniel, spoke to our group at her village. She said she and her friends saw what we did. She told us how deeply our actions had touched them. Tears welled up in her eyes as she related how moved they all were. She said they had never seen anything like it and would never forget it. I have chosen to include a few of the sites and experiences I had during this most interesting time in Judea and Samaria. As part of the tour, I visited the site that still marks the spot where the Tabernacle stood at Shiloh.

The Bible states the first Tabernacle was erected after the Jews entered Israel following the exodus from Egypt and the 40 years of living in the Sinai. Joshua 18:1 states, "The whole congregation of the children of Israel assembled together at Shiloh and erected there the Tent of Assembly, and the land was conquered before them."

Foundation stones of the Tabernacle

The Tabernacle remained at Shiloh for 369 years, according to the Talmud.[76]

Mission in Hebron

Although we had been informed the morning we were to go into Hebron that the IDF had refused us entry due to sniper fire there the previous night, Sondra Baras, leader of Christian Friends of Israeli Communities, gained the necessary permission to visit

---

[76]New World Encyclopedia, (n.d.) "Ahijah HaShiloni." Retrieved from www.newworldencyclopedia.org/entry/Ahijah_HaShiloni.

Two Mission Trips to the Land

Hebron. Besides riding in a bulletproof bus, we also had an IDF military escort that day. My heart literally leaped (and wept) at the opportunity to visit this ancient burial site of Abraham and Sarah, Isaac and Rebecca, Jacob and Leah, but that was not the reason I was going.

Hebron is a sister city to Jerusalem and is the oldest of the two. Machpelah, the burial site of the Patriarchs, is located in the caves at Hebron. We went to show support and solidarity to the Israeli community living there despite the dangers to honor God's covenant promise to them. I felt it was the height of importance that we go and show solidarity with those brave souls. Not one moment was I afraid.

Not one moment did I doubt our purpose in going because I knew it was God's heart that we show our solidarity to the small, Jewish community in Hebron.

We met with a local Jewish Rabbi at Machpelah within the confines of Herod's Memorial structure built over the burial caves. He walked us through the history of the Arab conflict, including the massacre of Hebron's Jews in 1929.

In 2001, it looked like a ghost town because there were no cars or people on the streets. The only children I saw were playing on a side street well below the road level, which gave some protection from sniper fire but allowed us visitors, to look down on them as they played outside their apartments. Our guide told us these families are cut from a different cloth from most. They are fearless because they believe they must occupy this city. They think they have a spiritual-legal ground (rights) to occupy the land that God gave their forefathers who are buried there.

About 700 years ago, the Muslim Mamelukes conquered Hebron, declared the Machpelah structure a mosque, and forbade entry to Jews who were not allowed past the seventh step on a staircase outside the building. Upon the liberation of Hebron in 1967, the IDF's Chief Rabbi, the late Major-General Rabbi Shlomo Goren, was the first Jew to enter the Cave of Machpelah. Since then, Jews have been struggling to regain their prayer rights at the site, still run by the Muslim Waqf (Religious Trust) that took control during the Arab conquest. Many restrictions are imposed on Jewish prayers and customs at the Tomb of the Patriarchs despite the site's significance, primacy, and sanctity in Jewish heritage and history.[77]

Today, they still cannot pray inside the building because the Muslims have claimed Machpelah as a mosque. They are allowed inside the room commemorating Isaac and Rebecca only on high holy days but never inside the room where the cenotaph (tomb representing the remains of Jacob) is located.

While in Hebron, we were made aware and later given a brochure pertaining to the Caves of Machpelah.[78]

The mandate preventing access to Jacob and Leah's room came about after the Arabs found out that the Jews had lowered a girl through the hole in the rock flooring in search of the underground caves believed to be the burial site of their ancestors. It is reported that General Moshe Dayan lowered the girl into the caves, upon gaining access to the caves after the war of 1967, not realizing there was another easier access from outside Herod's Structure. The sages say this is also the burial place of Adam and Eve, which means that Adam and Eve, Abraham and Sara, Isaac and Rebecca, Jacob and Leah are all buried in the caves. And therefore it is called Kiryat Arba—the city of the four—because four couples were buried there.[79]

The One New Man

I am happy to report that my most cherished experience in Israel was to unite with the people on the other side of the olive tree—the natural branches. There is a growing population of Messianic Jews in Israel. Also, the door is open for us to express to the unbelieving Jew the unconditional love of Jesus.

More Jews have come to know Jesus as their Messiah in the last 20

---

[77]The Jewish Virtual Library, (n.d.). Hebron: Tomb of the Patriarchs (*Ma'arat HaMachpelah*). Retrieved from http://www.jewishvirtuallibrary.org/jsource/Judaism/machpelah.html.

[78]Entering the Caves of Machpelah by Noam Arnon. July 20, 2006. Retrieved from: http://www.hebron.com/english/article.php?id=282.

[79]Jewish Encyclopedia. MachPelah. Retrieved from www.jewishencyclopedia.com/articles/10248-machpelah.

years than in the last 2000! The veil is slowly lifting, and we Gentile Christians have an important role to play, which is clearly defined in Romans 10:19 and 11:14. In John 17:20-21, Jesus was asking His Father for Jews and Gentiles to become one body of believers in Him. "So that the world may believe and be convinced that You have sent me." And the second half contains the prayer, "So that the glory that is on (You) the Father will be on them!" (AMP)

The early church had it and lost it when Constantine severed it from its roots. The Gentile church effectively tore itself away from being a part of the One New Man Paul talked about, and Jesus prayed about. The Reformation did not go back far enough to reconnect the church to its original Jewish roots. The mystery of the church, that spiritual connection between Jew and Gentile remained lost, but it is coming back.

Judy in front of Machpelah

2001 | Hebron, outside the Tombs of the Patriarchs

God's Heart—God's Fire

Thank God Christians now have the opportunity to do ministry work among these precious Jewish people (separated unto God) from whom our salvation and faith have come. God is restoring the Church to its Jewish roots and the Jewish people to their Messiah. And as the oil from that rich olive tree begins to flow, the miracles, signs, and wonders from the times of the New Testament beginning at Shavuot (Pentecost) are coming back into the body of Christ.

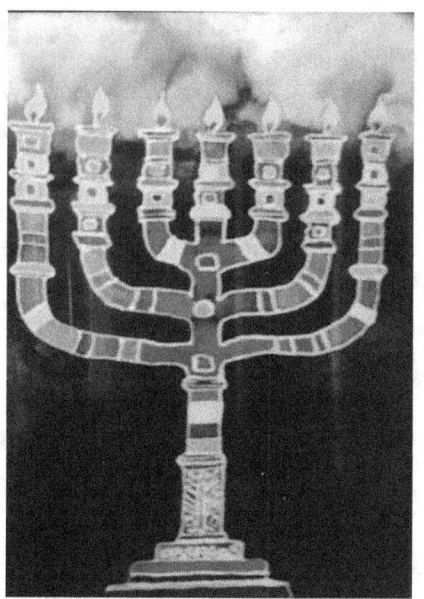

The Vision: Lampstand for the Nations
Judy's Multicolored Menorah - The One New Man

Chapter 22

My Turkish Friend

Book of Revelation Tour

A few months after I returned home from Israel, I found myself flying into Athens, Greece.[80] I spent two days in Athens, touring the ancient ruins of the Acropolis, Mars Hill, and Corinth. Afterward, my group sailed on a cruise ship, the World Renaissance, to the Rhodes ancient island. The ancient city, with its fortified rock walls, reminded me of Jerusalem's old city. I spent the day wandering around mostly by myself, soaking up the relic's unique atmosphere from the past.

From Rhodes, we went on to Patmos, the island where the Apostle John lived in exile. We saw the hollowed-out place in the cave of the grotto wall where John is reported to have rested his head. We left the ship at Izmir, Turkey (the ancient city of Smyrna), and visited the ruins of Ephesus, Sardis, Pergamum, Thyatira, Philadelphia, and Laodicea.

---

[80]Names in this divine appointment have been changed to protect the believers in this story.

New Revelations

I want to inject some of my revelations from this very defining trip. Defining in that I met and befriended Allison.[81] Allison and I walked in the ancient ruins of the churches where Paul walked and preached the gospel. Corinth and Ephesus are foremost in my mind whenever I think about this trip. There were defining moments like seeing stone bunnies in the rubble of the ancient temple of the fertility goddess, Artemis, at Ephesus, and seeing a Menorah carved on a stone column in Corinth.

I had wondered if Paul was speaking to both Jew and Gentile when writing his letters to believers in Corinth, and seeing the Menorah was very telling in that regard. Another moment came when our Turkish guide pointed to a spot between a grove of trees as we approached the ruins of Ephesus and said, "That is where Mary, the mother of Jesus, spent her last days. She died at Ephesus.

And I did not believe him. I had never heard what happened to Mary after Jesus was resurrected. Why would Mary move to Ephesus? I couldn't wrap my mind around the notion that Mary ever left Israel. But later, when I found out that John, the Revelator, did not die on the Island of Patmos, but died in Ephesus, it made sense. After all, the disciple whom Jesus loved was charged with looking after Mary, and it is only logical they would both wind up in the same place living out their last days together.

The trip brought other revelations as well. Christians have speculated that Paul might have been making prayer shawls instead of tents because no one lived in tents during that time period. Prayer shawls can form a kind of tent over the individual when placed over the head. However, I learned from our guide while I was in Corinth that Paul's father had a large tent factory, and the Apostle learned the trade from his father. Tents back then were made of goat hair and were used to cover the head to protect people from the elements while traveling. People used them on long journeys. Our Greek guide explained that there were no hotels to stay in while traveling at the time, so travelers had to carry their lodging with them.

---

[81] To protect her privacy, I have chosen to refer to her as Allison—not her real name.

Most were small, no larger than 20 inches wide, and everyone had one. Learning the trade from his father, Paul made the tents from time to time to support himself. He could also have made prayer shawls, but it seems unlikely.

Unhappy Camper

While still in Greece, something happened that quickly turned me into an unhappy camper. So I asked my heavenly Father, "Why am I here? I believe You called me to come on this trip, but why?" Expecting a mission outreach, I was stymied. We conducted one service while still in Athens, but the rest was purely a pilgrimage. And God answered! "*Turkey—it's in Turkey.* The reason for your trip is in Turkey." We spent two days in Izmir and then flew back to Istanbul.

Right on Cue

And right on cue. God showed up and showed Himself strong. In the early morning of our last day, we were taken to the world-famous Blue Mosque in Istanbul. I lost track of my friend Allie[82] who, like me, declined to go inside the site because of having to take off our shoes, which was the same as bowing to a false god. I had to visit the outdoor facilities, so we separated but planned to meet on the other side of the mosque where our team would exit the building. When I got there, there was no sign of Allie, but I noticed two women were also waiting for our group, and they were talking to a young Turkish lad about 18 years of age.

I came upon the scene when they asked him if he went into the mosque five times a day to pray. He sheepishly said no because he was not good enough. He explained that the night before, he had been led into impurity by drinking and partying with friends, during which time a young woman from Holland had tried to seduce him, and when he tried to explain why he would not have sex with her, she mocked and laughed at him. He seemed upset that he could not make a foreigner understand why he would not do it. Without giving it a second thought, I jumped into the conversation and said,

---

[82] Not her real name.

"I know why. Because it's wrong, it's just plain wrong!" At that point, the conversation became a dialogue between the two of us. I sensed an immediate connection. The young man remained with us and continued to talk. He asked why people continue to do the wrong things when they know the right thing to do. Then he began to talk about how empty he felt inside.

At that moment, the Holy Spirit of God rose in me, and a witness began to roll out of my mouth. I was amazed to hear myself say, "I can tell you what that is. We are all born with a hole inside us that only the One true and living God can fill." I was mindful that to him, Allah was god, so I used the phrase "the One true and living God." I continued by saying, "At different times in our lives, these two friends and I prayed a prayer that changed our lives, and the One true, and living God came inside and filled that hole." I told him about Jesus Christ, His only Son, Who suffered and died on the Cross for us so that through His blood, we can be cleansed from our sins and made pure enough to come into God's presence. I shared the entire gospel message with him the best way that I could. Then, when I looked up at his face, I was shocked to see him brushing tears away from his eyes. I instantly realized this moment would never come again, so I said, "Would you like to pray that same prayer we prayed right now?" And to my amazement, he said, "Yes!"

I led him in the sinner's prayer, and he repeated it after me, word for word. Afterward, He patted his stomach and said that he no longer felt empty inside. I left him knowing God had something very special in mind for his life. I told him that he needed to get a Bible and read it because it is the living word, the bread of life. I turned to my teammates sitting on the steps and asked if they had a Bible. They shook their heads, no. Later, they told me they could not believe I had thought to give him a Bible. I had momentarily forgotten the warnings about sharing the gospel or giving a Bible to anyone in Turkey.

Earlier, before we disembarked the World Renaissance to set foot on Turkish soil, we were told to get rid of all tracts and Christian religious material targeted at Muslims. We were told if we gave anyone a Bible or any other Christian literature, we would go to jail. I still remember the exact words of that warning. Quoting the board

My Turkish Friend

game Monopoly, our leader said, "If you talk to Muslims about Jesus or give them a tract or Bible, you will not pass 'Go,' you will go directly to jail." Only if they engaged us in conversation could we bring up the gospel of Jesus Christ, and in that respect, I was on solid ground. But the Bible? No.

The boy gave me his father's business card, so we were able to get the boy's contact information to two different groups of missionaries in that city, then we trusted God with the rest.

Just before we parted, I snapped a picture of him. Later on, I learned that when we talked with him, the friend Allison, whom I had lost track of, had bumped into another lady from our group and had stopped to pray for Muslims. Without realizing it, they interceded on my behalf and for the soul of that young Turkish boy.

Just talking to this man about the Lord had made us (and him) vulnerable. I remember hearing later that two home Bible study groups in Turkey were infiltrated, and the believers were bludgeoned to death in the name of Allah before the police could get there. Today, I pray for the safety of my new young brother in Christ. I pray he grows in the knowledge and understanding of the truth of God's word. When the two ladies and I parted with the young man, we were about as giddy as little children over what the Lord had done in his heart.

But that exuberance faded (momentarily) when we arrived at our next destination. Within walking distance of the Blue Mosque, we visited an ancient Catholic Church. I recall our tour guide telling us it was one of the oldest known Christian churches. The Ottoman Turks desecrated and defaced it by covering the interior walls and ceiling with Islamic symbols and writings in Arabic. I remember how the feeling of offense pierced my soul when I saw a huge Islamic seal superimposed over the beautiful Christian images on the high ceiling. We felt such a strong sense of abomination that some team members became nauseated. Along with a few others, I just sat down apart from the tour group leader and waited to leave.

I liked the Turkish people in general and found that most of them also liked Americans. Everyone we met was friendly toward us. The Turks are descendants of northern Europeans. They are not originally of Arab descent. I remember not understanding their currency, and three times I gave shopkeepers too much money when I tried to pay for an item. Each time they corrected me and gave me back my proper change. I would never have known the difference.

I recall a report from the wife of a U.S. military man based in Turkey who said that after the town's people heard the news about the 9/11 attack, the native Turks came out and surrounded the homes of the Americans to protect them. I was also surprised by seeing the Israeli flag flying among the other nation's flags outside our hotel in Istanbul because most Middle Eastern Muslim countries do not recognize Israel's right to exist. Unfortunately, the Book of Revelation reveals that Turkey is one of the countries that will fight against Israel at the battle of Armageddon. Today, Turkey no longer supports Israel and has sided with Iran against her.

In conclusion, the most defining moment and purpose of this trip happened when I came face to face with that young Muslim boy who was seeking the one true God Who is not Allah. And meeting Allison, who like me, was being pulled forward toward our destiny in the heart of Rome.

My Turkish Friend

Part V

Identification Repentance

CHAPTER 23

AUSCHWITZ, POLAND

In 2005, I sat in the audience at CBU's Jewish Roots Conference at Montreat, North Carolina, listening to Dr. Howard Morgan's[83] talk about his experience as a speaker at the first Holocaust to Living Hope Conference in Poland. He spoke about two brothers whose village lies on the Sola River across from the Nazi death camps of Auschwitz and Auschwitz II Birkenau. Pastor Stanislaw Gawel does a pro-Israel conference in Zilina, Slovakia, each year. Both brothers are ministers of the gospel and operate Shalom Ministries.

When Communism fell in 1989, they dedicated their lives to helping Jewish people in every way possible. As Dr. Morgan shared how the experience of being at the Nazi death camps at Oswiecim (Auschwitz) affected him, I became especially interested in these two brothers. Could they be the same two that were my teammates on the

---

[83]Dr. Howard Morgan is an internationally renowned prophetic teacher.... A Jewish believer in the Messiah Jesus since 1971, he planted and pastored churches in New York City from 1976 to 1987. Since 1987 he has been traveling in a full time prophetic and teaching ministry, establishing and overseeing churches and ministries, and pastoring pastors. He is a gifted communicator who is able to present scriptural truths clearly and precisely, so that the principles of the Kingdom of God are plainly understood and easily applied. His ministry is often accompanied by clear demonstrations of the revelatory gifts of the Holy Spirit. Retrieved from www.oneinmessiahministries.org/index.php/resources/ministry-links.

Mission of Solidarity Trip to Israel five years earlier? The moment Dr. Morgan said he planned to take a group of people to participate in the first annual conference on identification repentance, I was quickened to the core. I raised my hand before he finished the sentence inviting those in the audience to go with him and his wife, Janet. After the service, I rushed up to ask about the two brothers and to sign up. Pastors Stanislaw and Roman Gawel were indeed the same two men I had met on the 2001 trip.

Two Pages in a Book

In preparation for the trip to Poland, I picked up a book entitled *The Holocaust and the Christian World* [84] that I had purchased at the Holocaust Museum bookstore in 2001. I had never read it; it was residing on my bookcase gathering dust, so I plucked it off the shelf and opened it to find information jumping out at me. I already had a general knowledge of the subject matter, but these pages were different. They revealed a story about the Huguenot congregation in France that saved hundreds of Jewish children during the Holocaust. The pastor and congregation were given the same status as the Ten Boom family. In a paragraph about people risking their lives to save the Jews, the Ten Boom family and the French Huguenot congregation were mentioned in the same paragraph, almost in the same breath.

At the dinner table one night, I happened to mention to Dr. Morgan's wife, Janet, that my ancestors were Huguenots, and to my surprise, she said, "Oh, they were the good guys." Janet is co-pastor of Howard Morgan Ministries and Kingdom Ministries International. Her comment stuck with me and prompted me to search the web after I got home to see if I could find any link between the Huguenots and the Jews. When I got home and began my search, I was astounded to discover there was a link. The article by Armand

---

[84] Rittner, C., Smith, S.D., Steinfeldt, I., (2000). *The Holocaust and the Christian World*. New York: Continuum.

Laferrere *The Huguenots, the Jews, and Me*[85] was an eye-opener. It was life-changing and prompted me to investigate further into the philo-Semitism of my ancestors and ultimately led to my writing this book.

What are the odds of opening a book to the very page containing information that affected me for the rest of my life? How could it have been a coincidence? In my life's journey, I have learned to count such coincidences as more than happenstance; I count them as godly interventions.

Death Factories

I flew into Warsaw to meet the American team in August of 2007. The team was comprised of 7 Americans and 31 others from various parts of the world. Our visit to the death camps exposed us to some truly shocking history that was extremely personal to each of us, and no two people experienced the realities in the same way.

This trip reminded me of hearing Benjamin Netanyahu speak to a room full of Christians in Ariel, Israel in 2001, telling us that the Israelites believe the bones of their kinsmen stacked up like cord wood in the Holocaust refers to the passage in Ezekiel 37:1-14 that describes the "dry bones" living again. Netanyahu was referring to the modern state of Israel and how, after the Holocaust, the nations were moved to agree to the formation of a Jewish homeland.

He also said that the scroll with this verse about dry bones living was the only part of God's word that survived the destruction of the ancient synagogue at Masada after the Roman invasion. The fragment was discovered stuck in between cracks in the old synagogue stones after it came back into Jewish hands in the 1967 war.

Many striking examples of the horrors inflicted on the Jewish people are memorialized at the Polish Museum in Warsaw. I watched one film clip after another archived by the Nazis as well as a longer videotape was shown to us by the Museum guide. There in black and

---

[85]Laferrere, A. (2006). "The Huguenots, the Jews, and Me: A Tale of French Philo-Semitism." Shalem Press: AzureOnline, Autumn 5767 / 2006, no. 26. Retrieved from http://azure.org.il/article.php?id=43. The original article in its entirety was removed from the Internet after Laferrere's death in 2013 but portions of it can still be found by googling The Huguenots, The Jews and Me by Armand Laferrere.

white were actual, moving scenes recorded by the Germans as they inflicted terror in so many horrible ways. On the wall were scenes of children dancing around bullets being fired at their feet while they begged for bread in the Warsaw Ghetto. I filmed the silent moving pictures with my own camcorder, but after I got home, I deleted all of them out of respect.

The conference that brought us to Poland took place at Oswiecim; a town renamed Auschwitz by the Nazis. Auschwitz II Birkenau was located just a few miles away. They were two of the most famous death factories in World War II. We visited various historical places in Warsaw and Krakow before journeying to the camps.

Dr. Morgan prepared the team for the intensity of darkness and depravity we were going to experience in Auschwitz before we left Krakow. It was hard to imagine things could get any worse. He suggested we put on the garment of praise for the spirit of heaviness that we were about to encounter (see Isaiah 61:3).

That night in Krakow, we became one in the Spirit and interceded for one another. We entered into a time of praise and worship, relying completely on God's power to see us through. The Bible says that "He [God] will guard and keep in perfect and constant peace all [those] whose mind [both its inclination and its character] is stayed on Him because he commits himself to Him, leans on Him, and hopes confidently in Him" (Isaiah 26:3-4 AMP) paraphrased. Our team became one as Jew and Gentile carried out a singular purpose, that is, effectively becoming the One New Man (see Eph. 2:15) in the Lord Jesus Christ/Yeshua Ha Mashiach as we listened to the conference speakers in Auschwitz and saw the horrors first-hand.

Auschwitz and Sunflowers

One woman in our team had a dream about carrying sunflowers to the death camps, and the next day she bought sunflowers and brought them with her. So we laid them at various locations at both Auschwitz I and II- Birkenau. The "Selection Point" is one of them. There are no cemeteries, no gravestones. There is no point of contact that mourners can show respect to and honor the dead victims; by placing flowers at their graves, we laid a single sunflower representing each grave where the mass murders took place. By doing so, we were showing honor and respect to the thousands who died there. In his book: "*The Sunflower: On the possibilities and limits on forgiveness,*"[86] Author Simon Wiesenthal, Holocaust survivor, and famous Nazi hunter, speaks about his feelings about seeing sunflowers growing and blooming, (planted and well maintained by the German population) on top of fallen SS soldier's graves in German military cemeteries. The sunflower became, to him, a symbol of honor shown the fallen Nazi SS soldier. So, we honored their murdered dead victims by placing a single sunflower on the ground.

I was surprised to learn about the industrial companies that aided the murder of six million Jews by supplying the Nazis with the means to do what they did. Nothing occurred in a vacuum. I think about Bayer aspirin's role in making the cyanide pellets used in the death camps. To this day, I react negatively whenever I see bottles of Bayer aspirin.

Four Atrocities

Four atrocities followed me home and would not let go of me for a very long time. They haunted me and invaded my thoughts for many months. Sharing them here reflects my journey through that emotional pain.

At the Jewish Museum in Warsaw, I saw a video of SS (Schutzstaffel) officers forcing young Jewish virgins into a Mikvah (a Jewish ritualistic cleansing pool of water) while laughing and pointing as they were filming them in full frontal nudity. The Nazis were using the cleansing pool for the opposite reason, that is, to defile them. They were trying to make people dedicated to keeping themselves clean and pure before a holy and righteous God feel unclean and unholy. That is why these women needed to declare they would not be shamed by it. The video lingers in my mind to this day because, as a woman, I empathized. I felt ashamed and humiliated as if it were happening to me.

---

[86]See holocaust survivor and famous Nazi hunter, Simon Wiesenthal's book, "The Sunflower: On the Possibilities and Limits of Forgiveness."

Living Waters

The Jewish Mikvah is related to the origin of our Christian baptism; it is symbolic of the washing away of our sins and passing through the water to newness of life. The Nazis ridiculed and attempted to mock the God of the Jews in other ways as well. For example, the tops of ghetto walls in Krakow were made to look like Torah Scrolls. I am reminded of how much this added to their distress and pain, just as their jailers knew it would. In Judaism, the Torah Scrolls are treated with utmost respect and care. The Jewish people handle them like they are touching the very words of God. They are stored in a central place in the Synagogue in special ornate curtained-off cabinets called the Aron Kodesh ("Holy Ark"). The Nazis knew this and did it to mock the Jewish God. Again, there was much empathy on my part, for I honor and cherish the same book.

At the first camp in Auschwitz (formerly used as a Polish military base), we were taken inside a building that existed for the sole purpose of torture not only for Jews but also for Gypsies and political prisoners. Just outside this building was the Place of Death, the wall against which the Germans shot those who survived the torture rooms. The most horrific place in my mind was the small brick enclosure in the torture house, approximately four by four feet, in which men were stripped of their clothes and forced to stand naked, jam-packed against each other, unable to move until they died of hunger or thirst. The catwalk above allowed the Nazis a bird's eye view of the dying men. As we walked on that same catwalk above the cubicle, I tried to imagine their pain and horror at spending days in such a state before dying.

The image of two 12-year-old boys with their genitals cut off simply to see their reaction still haunts me. According to our guide, they survived the war and spent the rest of their lives in an insane asylum. Perhaps it affected me more deeply than some of the other acts because of the dehumanizing aspect of them standing before a camera stripped naked with their horrible wounds exposed.

It was reflected in their eyes; they looked as if their spirit and soul had already ceased to exist. Even today, I can hardly bear visiting that image in my mind's eye.

The Wind of the Spirit

Before we left Warsaw, we visited the Warsaw Ghetto Monument. We were surprised to arrive at the same time as an official Israeli government wreath-laying ceremony to commemorate the Warsaw Ghetto Uprising. It consisted of IDF soldiers and military officials. When their commander learned of our purpose in Poland—to attend the Holocaust to Hope Conference and participate in identification repentance on behalf of the Christian world—they invited us to participate in their commemorative ceremony.

A member of our team saw someone selling flowers nearby and ran to buy an arrangement for us to lay at the base of the monument alongside the Star of David wreath to be placed there by the Israeli defense force.

Star of David Wreath placed at the Warsaw Ghetto Monument

Four of the Holocaust to Hope team, representing the UK, USA, Poland, and Germany, presented the floral arrangement during the ceremony. IDF soldiers who were lined up in rows on each side of the monument stood at attention. The Star of David wreath passed through the line of soldiers standing at attention, as did the floral arrangement we presented. Afterward, we got the opportunity to express our love and support of Israel and the Jewish people to the IDF. More importantly, a few in the group got the opportunity to explain why we love them. That begs the question that my readers will find the answer to in Romans Chapter 11. We came away rejoicing because we believed our unplanned meeting with the Israeli military leaders and IDF soldiers to be a divine appointment (orchestrated by God). Was this just a happenstance? What are the odds of it being a coincidence?

The Holy Spirit of God moved in many ways and showed Himself strong during our mission to Poland. We all felt God was giving us a thumbs-up as witness and confirmation about our endeavor. After the memorial service was over, I wandered around with my camera and saw a dove sitting on the top of the ghetto monument watching us. For me, this dove was a sign of the Lord's presence.

In other places, we felt His presence in the strong winds that would come up during special moments like our prayer time at the Jewish cemetery in Warsaw. While we were praying, a powerful wind began to surge as if a storm was coming with no clouds in the sky, only to die down suddenly after the prayer was over. Days later, after it reoccurred under different but unique circumstances, did I remember the strength and suddenness of the wind that met us in the Warsaw Cemetery. We soon received ample confirmation that it really was the wind of the Spirit whom God was sending. Glory to God!

The retaining wall surrounding this graveyard was made from cemetery headstones taken by the Nazis from Jewish graves. Some were used as roadbeds while others, like the ones I saw surrounding the cemetery, became a retaining wall. Another example of God showing Himself strong was when the wind blew for no apparent reason at the Auschwitz II Birkenau Camp. Daniela was standing above the pit that contained bone fragments and human ashes, speaking words of repentance (in her native German language) into the camera and the open air above the pit when the wind suddenly began to blow. It is important to note that Daniela was chosen to be the one speaking at the site because she had the spiritual-legal ground to do it.

The supernatural significance of the wind's sudden appearance might have been missed had it not been for the cameraman filming Daniela's confession. His video camera had wind protection, yet he reported that he "heard the wind" inside his earphones. This was virtually impossible since the video camera was designed to filter out the wind so that it did not interfere with the sound recording.

However, during the interview with Daniela, he clearly heard the wind when she spoke into the heavens above the bone fragments in the ash pit. Dr. Morgan testified to this curious occurrence later that day at the conference. We believed it was a mighty wind from the Spirit of the living God that blew that morning at Auschwitz, and God wanted us to know it.

Blood Cries Out

The Russian army liberated the remaining prisoners at Auschwitz II Birkenau Poland, but not before the Nazis tried to cover their crimes by blowing up the gas chambers and crematorium to hide the evidence of their crimes. However, the Germans failed to destroy all traces of it before the Russians got there. The entire grounds and remnants of the buildings were left as they were found as a witness to the world of what the Germans had done.

In a previous document and conference sermon, Dr. Morgan testified that during his first visit to the death camps in Poland, he heard the blood of the murdered Jews crying out from the ground. He said it seemed crazy and impossible, but he heard them. When he took it to the Lord, the Holy Spirit told him that it was not the first time spilled blood of the saints had cried out from the ground. He was reminded that God heard Abel's blood cry out to Him after his brother slaughtered him. Genesis 4:10, "And [the Lord] said, 'What have you done? The voice of your brother's blood is crying to Me from the ground'" (AMP). At Fort Caroline and Matanzas, Florida, the blood of the Huguenot martyrs cried out from the ground, and God heard them as well.

The day that I left for Poland, I grabbed my land of Israel necklace and stuck it in my suitcase as an afterthought. Little did I know how important that necklace would be. I had purchased it from an IDF soldier in 2002. The soil inside the necklace was collected from all parts of Israel, put in a vial, and worn around the neck to remember God's love for Israel and the Jewish people.

The morning that we were about to board the bus leaving Krakow for Oswiecim, the Holy Spirit began speaking to my spirit. Though I did not understand it at the time, I knew in my heart and soul that

God wanted me to give the necklace to Dr. Morgan. I shared this with him on board the bus, confessing that all I knew was that God wanted me to give it to him. But, glory to God, Dr. Morgan knew! He later told me that the moment the necklace was put into his hand, he knew exactly what he was to do with it; at the Auschwitz II Birkenau death camp, he tossed the necklace into the ash pit. It was as if we were saying to the dead, "We can't take your bones to Israel, but we can take a little bit of Israel to you." Only then did I comprehend God's divine purpose in nudging me to take the land of Israel necklace to Poland. I believe that my little vial of soil from the Holy Land and identification repentance by all those present at the selection point were part of God's plan to redeem the Holocaust by cleansing the ground and dedicating it back to Him. Glory be to God for His accomplishments in the realm of the Spirit when that vial containing the Holy Land of Israel was left there in August 2007.

Torah Scroll on Ghetto wall in Krakow

Auschwitz, Poland

The following year at the 2008 Holocaust to Hope Conference, Pastor Werner Oder, whose father was second in command of the *SS Einsatzgruppen* (mobile killing squads) training school in Rabka, Poland, asked to join the conference team. From Dr. Morgan's newsletter, I offer the following account.[87]

> *It was here, at the selection point, the SS troops directly responsible for murdering over 1 million Jewish men, women and children, trained. It was through a series of divine appointments that Dr. Morgan and Janet met Pastor Werner, heard his amazing testimony of salvation and deliverance from the demonic strongholds of his Austrian families' Nazi history, and his call to stand with the Jewish people against their enemies. It was here that we led the Communion at the Selection Point service to honor all those who were massacred.*
>
> *As part of this time of prayer and repentance, Pastor Werner and his wife, Avril, washed our feet as they wept over the sins committed by his ancestors and all who were responsible for the atrocities of the Holocaust. For Janet and me, these were moments beyond description. As we stood together in prayer, we were shocked to see Pastor Werner suddenly holding a cross he had fashioned out of pieces of barbed wire from the camp fence over our heads. Pastor Werner's grandfather had actually erected the barbed wire for the Nazis. He held up the cross he had fashioned out of part of this fence and expressed his desire to repent and compensate for his ancestor's part in the atrocities.*
>
> *He had cut the barbed wire down with his bare hands and formed a cross out of it. He believed he had the legal ground to do this because it was "his people" who built the death camps.*
>
> *The cross he fashioned symbolizes both the horrors of the Holocaust and the only thing in the world that can redeem us; the cross upon which our Jewish Messiah died to bring redemption to all mankind.*

---

[87]Morgan, H. (2008). Howard Morgan Ministries Newsletter, HMM Connect. Retrieved from http://www.howardmorganministries.org.

As we stood together at this place of evil and death with the barbed wire cross over our heads, with Pastor Werner; an Austrian son of a mass murderer and a Jewish believer in Jesus, we formed a living symbol of what that cross had accomplished and will yet accomplish; true forgiveness and redemption—the One New Man.

As we held this cross over our heads together, people began to point to the sky above us. There, directly overhead, a cross formed in the sky. It looked like it could have been formed by two airplanes leaving an exhaust trail, but there were no planes insight, and it only appeared when we were holding that barbed wire cross up and praying for God's redemptive purposes to be completed! Beloved friends, it is impossible for us to put into words what that experience was like and what God is doing through this ministry in Poland.

In conclusion, Pastor Werner Oder went to the site and cut the barbed wire because, as the son of the one who put it there, he had the spiritual-legal ground to do so. This coincides with my message about the legal ground.

Blessed be the God and Father of our Lord Jesus Christ, the Father of mercies and God of all comfort. Who comforts us in all our affliction that we may be able to comfort those who are in any affliction with the comfort with which we ourselves are comforted by God (2 Corinthians 1:3-4).

To see the photo of this amazing phenomena, go to Howard Morgan Ministries and click on "Communion at the Selection Point."

CHAPTER 24

REMEMBERING THE HOLOCAUST

The shedding of the blood of the Jewish people while the church stood by as though paralyzed in WWII brings me back to a time when the shedding of blood was done by the church.

August 24, 1572, was the date of the infamous St. Bartholomew's Day Massacre in France. On that day, over 400 years ago, the most horrifying holocausts in history began. The glorious Reformation, begun in Germany on October 31, 1517, had spread to France and was joyfully received. A great change came over the people as industry and learning began to flourish, and as the truth spread, over a third of the population embraced the Reformed Christian faith.

However, alarm bells began to ring at the Vatican! France was Rome's eldest daughter and main pillar—the chief source of money and power. King Pepin of the Franks (the father of Charlemagne) had given the Papal States to the Pope almost 1,000 years earlier. The clergy owned almost half of the real estate in the country.

Meanwhile, back in Paris, the King of France and his court spent their time drinking, reveling, and carousing. The court spiritual adviser—a Jesuit priest—urged them to massacre the Protestants as penance for their many sins! To catch the Christians off-guard, every token of peace, friendship, and ecumenical goodwill was offered.

Suddenly and without warning, the devilish work commenced. In Paris, the French soldiers and the Roman Catholic clergy fell upon the unarmed people, and blood flowed like a river throughout the country. Men, women, and children fell in heaps before the mobs and the bloodthirsty troops. In one week, almost 100,000 Protestants perished. The rivers of France were so filled with corpses that for many months no fish were eaten. In the valley of the Loire, wolves came down from the hills to feed upon the decaying bodies of the Frenchmen. The list of massacres was as endless as the list of the dead!

Many were imprisoned, and others sent as slaves to row the king's ships, but some were able to escape to other countries. The massacres continued for centuries. The best and brightest people fled to Germany, Switzerland, England, Ireland, and eventually America and brought their incomparable manufacturing skills with them. France was ruined. Wars, famine, disease, and poverty finally led to the French Revolution—the Guillotine, the Reign of Terror, and the fall of the Roman Catholic Monarchy, etc.

When news of the Massacre reached the Vatican, there was jubilation. Cannons roared, bells rung, and a special commemorative medal was struck to honor the occasion. The Pope commissioned Italian artist Vasari to paint a mural of the Massacre that still hangs in the Vatican!

Remembrance

An Eyewitness Account of the Saint Bartholomew's Day Massacre by François Dubois | From the Musée Cantonal Des Beaux-Arts, Lausanne, Switzerland

Medal struck by Emperor Gregory XIII (1572-1585) to commemorate the slaughter of over 100,000 French Christians!

CHAPTER 25

ROME AND GENERATIONAL REDEMPTION

"Is this seat taken?"

I recognized her the moment she boarded my bus. I welcomed Allison to my seat while saying a silent "Thank You, Lord" for bringing her across my path again. It was the month of October in 2004, and I was in Italy visiting Florence and Venice with outreach in Rome. Once again, I had secured a private room for myself to avoid the pitfalls of rooming with a stranger, and in retrospect, I see that need to do so was the way my Father had of arranging and cultivating a friendship with this special lady who also traveled alone. She had been my seat partner during a previous trip, and for her to be assigned to my bus again out of several other buses was no happenstance. No accident. No coincidence. The close spiritual bond we had established in Greece and Turkey made our relationship in Italy bound to blossom and grow quickly.

One of the most important spiritual events ever to occur in my life took place in Rome. Not only did I participate in evangelistic outreaches on downtown streets in the heart of the city, but Allison and I became part of a secret mission our Father had planned and orchestrated from the beginning of our friendship.

Accidental Confession

I was standing outside the Roman Coliseum waiting for some team members to come out of the bathroom when I made an offhand remark to my old traveling buddy, Sandra, and her friend Patty.[88] I told them that because I was a descendant of French Huguenots, perhaps we should use the time to pray—hoping they understood what I meant. They caught the significance, and Sandra responded by saying, "Now all we need is someone who is descended from the Roman Catholic Church." At that time, I did not understand but learned later that they were looking for two team members to join in an *identification repentance ceremony.*

After this exchange at the Coliseum, Allison went to visit Pompeii while I stayed behind in order to go again with the outreach team to downtown Rome. That evening when we returned to our hotel, Allison and I had dinner together, I told her that Sandra and her friend, Patty, were looking for a descendant from the Roman Catholic Church in order to perform an identification repentance ceremony with me since my ancestors were French Huguenots. To my surprise, she began to cry. She told me that before she left to come on this trip, her Pastor had told her that her connection to the Roman Catholic Church would play a major role in what God was going to do there. I had no idea her family is Catholic, and that she is descended from both the Roman and the French Catholic Churches. She said she had been waiting for our leader to ask if there was anyone who had Catholic ancestors. Her ancestral roots go back hundreds of years—as do mine. We knew what we had to do. She and I met with those unique ladies in their hotel room at 8:00 pm that night.

Our Calling to Rome

Both Allison and I had had previous teaching about identification repentance. Making a verbal confession (identifying the atrocities) asking for and receiving forgiveness of them, breaks the generational curses that have been passed down through the ages from bloodguilt. I remember reading JoAnne Meeks' book, *Who Me? One Worship*

---

[88]Not their real names.

Warriors Journey through 'Special Forces' Training in the Army of God, I met this interesting lady at CBU's Judeo-Christian Conference (affectionately known as "Jewish Roots Conferences") in Macon Georgia, after my trip to Poland. JoAnne has Cherokee ancestry and is a representative of American Indigenous tribes (as am I). She and others of America's First Nation are obeying God's call on their lives to do certain things for Him to cleanse and purge some North American lands from blood defilement and to participate in His purpose of reconciliation and restoration.

"For our struggle is not against flesh and blood, but against the rulers, against the powers, against the world forces of this darkness, against the spiritual forces of wickedness in the heavenly places." (Ephesians 6:12 NASB) JoAnne states in her book, "The time has come (and long past due) to bring God's reconciliation and restoration to the land defiled by much bloodshed, injustice, broken covenants, and evil."[89]

Blood Guilt and DNA

In September of 2004, two hurricanes made landfall at Hutchinson Island on Florida's east coast. Both hurricanes, Frances and Jeanne, came ashore at the same location near Port St. Lucie, Florida. Hurricane Jeanne was a category 3, with maximum sustained winds of 120 miles an hour. Frances came ashore twenty-one days *prior to Jeanne*. It made landfall on the same island and caused nearly $9 Billion in damages as it swept up the coast.

During the onslaught, Matanzas was hit hard, and the upper layers of dirt and sand that had accumulated over the decades since Don Pedro Menendes slaughtered Jean Ribault and 500 others in the Huguenot massacre, was removed, scoured away by the hurricanes.

This small island is at an inlet below St. Augustine where an estimated 500 gallons of innocent blood were left to soak into the ground. Forensic scientists would agree that traces of their blood DNA is still there in the sand. I believe common sense would say the same. One human body contains approximately 1.25 gallons

---

[89]Meeks, J. (n.d.) *Tears in a Bottle*, Page 83.

(4.7 liters) of blood, and if there were 500 men killed on the Island of Matanzas, one could calculate how much blood soaked into the ground in that one location. Let us not forget that the "line in the sand" was drawn in one spot, behind a high hill still identifiable today by a marker.

When a sample of this subsoil was taken from this exact location in Florida, brought to Rome and placed in my hand, it became more than a curiosity, more than a little interesting. It was profound. It was powerful. Soil from the blood-soaked sand from Matanzas containing Huguenot blood DNA stoked the fires of my imagination. Seeing it provided me with images of the Huguenot colony, slaughtered for their faith.

Bloodguilt

A correlation can be drawn from the repentant cry of King David, "Deliver me from bloodguilt (blood guiltiness) and death, O God, the God of my salvation, and my tongue shall sing aloud of Your righteousness (Your rightness and Your justice)" (Psalm 51:14 AMP)

> *Bloodguilt, liability for punishment for shedding blood. The biblical concept of bloodguilt derives from the belief that deeds generate consequences and that sin, in particular, is a danger to the sinner. The most vivid examples of this belief appear in connection with unlawful homicide, where innocent blood (dam naki (naqi); Jonah 1:14) cries out for vengeance (Gen. 4:10), is rejected by the earth (Isa. 26:21; Ezek. 24:7), and pollutes it (Num. 35:33–34). Bloodguilt attaches to the slayer and his family (II Sam. 3:28ff) for generations (II Kings 9:26), and even to his city (Jer. 26:5), nation (Deut. 21:8), and land (Deut. 24:4) The concept of bloodguilt in the Bible pervades all sources, legal, narrative, and cultic.*[90]

The whole idea of delegated authority is scriptural and necessary for fulfilling God's purpose for His creation. But the issue to always

---

[90] *Jewish Virtual Library (n.d.)* Retrieved from http://www.jewishvirtuallibrary.org/jsource/judaica/ejud_0002_0003_0_03145.html.

keep in mind is that this authority is based on the power of Christ's blood. Most of us know that through His sacrifice on Calvary, we have been restored to God by the shedding of Jesus' blood. And although we have not received as yet that full and final entrance into God's presence, we still have His authority to enforce His victory rights at Calvary right now.

The Ceremony

Our Heavenly Father provided the right time, the right place, and the right spiritual ground for Allison and me, as descendants of the Huguenots and the Holy Roman Catholic church, to join together in the ceremony of identification repentance. God provided the spiritual, legal ground for us as their descendants to stand in the gap and speak for them. This is why blood lineage is so important and necessary for restoration of lands and territories defiled by bloodguilt to occur.

We sat together on a bed in Patty's and Sandra's room. First, Allison turned to me, and in a spirit of sorrow, verbally confessed and repented of the atrocities, persecutions, and crimes perpetrated on my ancestors, by her ancestors. And because of my blood (DNA) lineage, I found myself in a position to exercise the authority given me by the Lord Jesus Christ, by His redeeming blood, to forgive on behalf of my dead ancestors. And I did.

The Vatican

We stood in the gap, obeyed the call of God on our own lives to represent our ancestors. We were confident that we were following His will as we walked together to the Vatican the next morning carrying sand from Matanzas, Florida. However, I could not help but wonder if I would ever truly know what took place in the realm of the spirit that day. Clearly it was not about reconciling the Catholic and Protestant churches to each other. What happened was not a dream or vision. It was an event in time that had to mean something to God's people for a specific purpose. Why else would He put a call on both our lives?

Imagine my excitement when I learned that Spanish-speaking communities in Florida, Mexico and even Spain had begun inviting Dr. Howard Morgan, a Messianic Jewish believer to come speak to them about their Hebraic roots. The door that had been closed for centuries had cracked open ever so slightly for them to reconnect to the primitive roots of their faith. Praise God. A paradigm shift had occured. The process of restoring that which was lost when Constantine severed the church from its root had begun.

Generational Redemption

Prophet James Goll, whom I referred to in an earlier chapter on identification repentance, speaks from his online article: "Confessing Generational Sin—Another Look at Identification in Intercession."[91]

> *This is perhaps one of the highest and most overlooked aspects of true intercession. It is identifying with the needs of the people to such an extent that in your heart you seem to "become one with them." Out of a heart of compassion, contrition, and desperation, your heart pounds with the sufferings of others as though it were your own. As you receive the heart of the Father, by the spirit of revelation, it is your own. You identify with God's righteous judgments, His desire for mercy, the peoples' horrifying condition, and their sins, which block the way. Then, by choosing to be "one of them," and laying aside your own position, your heart is burdened by the Spirit of God and a cry of confession of sin, disgrace, failure, and humiliation quietly and sometimes dramatically pours forth from your heart unto the Lord. You carry away the blockage of sin, so as to open the way that God's promise might proceed forth.*

Dr. Goll reports that generational sins are a block that must be removed. He says,

> *We are not dealing with the sin or actions of the individual who is praying because that should already (have) been taken care of.*

---

[91]Goll, J. (2007). "Confessing Generational Sin—Another Look at Identification in Intercession." Retrieved from https://www.identitynetwork.net/articles-and-prophetic-words

The prayer is for the sin or condition of another or even of an entire nation!

Dr. Goll continues:

Demonic spirits have no true authority to influence an area without permission or legal basis first granted. Certain conditions give them the authority to set up a base of operations from whence they exercise their oppression.

The following are some of the areas Dr. Goll lists where confessing generational sins is a necessity:

A. *Idolatry: Ex. 20:1-5, Deut. 7:5, 25-26, 1 Cor. 10:19-20*

B. *Temples to Pagan Religions*

C. *Murder and the Shedding of Innocent Blood*

So ye shall not pollute the land wherein ye are: for blood it defileth the land: and the land cannot be cleansed of the blood that is shed therein, but by the blood of him that shed it. (Num. 35:33 KJV)

This can be taken one step further through Katie D'Sousa's teaching by showing how identification repentance (repenting on behalf of ancestors) can close these wounds in territories and persons and reclaim them for God. We can work effectively in the Spirit when we have legal ground. Principalities and powers of the air will recognize spiritual authority and must relinquish control once they realize that we are using the authority given to us by the blood and the resurrection of God's power. This authority gives precedent over matters generated through our hereditary lineage. Most importantly, our actions have to be instigated, directed, and guided by the power of the Holy Spirit. Never should one go it alone.

Different Times, Different Seasons, Different Era

Praise God. He is doing a new thing. The season of restoration is upon us. Dr. Howard Morgan of Kingdom Ministries International-Living Word Ministry explains it in a quote from Dr. John Garr:

The wind of the Holy Spirit is truly blowing across the world, bringing the biblical understandings of the Gospels to the forefront and into the hearts of all believers. In these end times, as the church age comes to a close, this reawakening is occurring in the lives of believers and cannot be traced to any single identifiable human source.

This worldwide restoration movement of our Hebraic heritage is truly what "the Spirit is saying to the church." We pray that the Lord will give each one of us ears to hear and the ability to understand.

CHAPTER 26

CLEANSING THE GROUND

Joseph Ben-Israel had a dream while in Vienna, Austria, and Dr. Howard Morgan had a dream while in Auschwitz, Poland. Both claimed to have literally heard the blood of holocaust victims crying out from the ground. Joseph Ben-Israel's dream was about the tragedy of the many children who died during the Holocaust. He said God wanted the names of the children to be remembered and that the ground had to be cleansed from the blood defilement in places (countries) where the murder of 6 million Jews took place. His trip to Linz, Austria (Chapter 15), was to encourage Austrian Christians to stand up to the Austrian government about tearing down Hitler's birthplace.

The Austrian government finally decided, after years of debate and legal wrangling to revamp:—to change the visual image of the building by updating and making it more modern. They plan to turn it into a police station in order to save it from becoming a meeting place for neo-nazi sympathizers. The Austrian government placed a memorial at the site in front of Salzburger Vorstadt 15, Braunau am Inn, Upper Austria, where Adolf Hitler was born in 1889. The memorial was not a memorial to him but a stone placed in honor of and in memory of the victims of the Nazis.

Dr. Morgan takes people from all over the world to the selection point in Poland (Auschwitz II Birkenau), where the Nazis' delivered Jews for selection, instant death, or the work camps. During the Holocaust to Hope Conference at the same selection point, Christians gather annually to participate in an identification repentance ceremony about the murder of Jews whose blood cries out from the ground. It is both Joseph Ben-Israel and Dr. Howard Morgan's testimony that God told them that He wants the ground "defiled by bloodguilt" cleansed, redeemed for His glory. This is being achieved through identification repentance and remembrance ceremonies, one heart at a time.

From the St. Bartholomew Day's Massacre in France to Fort Caroline and Matanzas, Florida, in America, the blood of victims carrying Abraham's seed cries out from the ground, and God is letting us know that He hears.

For His Glory

Behold, to obey is better than sacrifice. And to heed is better than the fat (sacrifice) of rams. 1 Samuel 5:22

Dr. Howard Morgan carries the blood of Yeshua/Jesus (by the indwelling power of His Holy Spirit) to the selection point in the form of Holy Communion, where the most horrific crimes against God's people (Abraham's seed) occurred. Joseph Ben-Israel carried the blood of Yeshua/Jesus (by the indwelling power of His Holy Spirit) to Linz, Austria, the birthplace of the one who instigated and carried out such evil against Abraham's seed.

Allison and I by the indwelling power of His Holy Spirit carried the blood of Yeshua/Jesus to the place where the crimes against Abraham's seed originated. I believe these were not happenstances but designated times and callings for such a time as this.

Epilogue

Wrapping It Up

The Hand Print

On March 6, 2001, I had a head-on collision at an intersection directly in front of the hospital where my mother lay gravely ill in ICU. The man in the car that I hit was uninjured and permitted to leave the scene, but I was taken to the emergency room. My car was totaled beyond repair.

Upon impact, I felt as if I was being held in place. At the same time, I felt external pressure on my sternum right underneath my right breast. My body did not come into contact with any objects in the car. My head did not jerk forward or backward—and the airbag did not deploy. The next day, I checked myself expecting to find bruises made by the seatbelt. Still, I only found one injury—a roundish one underneath my right breast with marks extending out from its edge toward my right side.

A day or two later, as I looked at it in front of the mirror, puzzled by its strange shape, I happened to place my left hand over it and was amazed to find a perfect fit! The bruise was the shape of a handprint! Finally, I accepted the fact that an angel had protected me from serious bodily harm. I asked God why, and He said, "The seatbelt would not have held." I remembered then that an unseen force restrained me when the seatbelt did not clamp down upon impact. It moved with me as the upper part of my body plunged forward and to the right of the steering wheel, during which time my head came within inches of crashing against the dashboard. The force restraining me was so strong that I suffered excruciating pain in my chest for weeks. That night, I was wearing a necklace that I had purchased in Israel. The words written in Hebrew said, "The name of the Lord is a strong tower; the righteous runs into it and is safe" (Proverbs 18:10). I had taken off two other necklaces before hastily grabbing that one to wear. To my surprise, the male nurse attending me in the emergency room pointed to my necklace and asked if I was Jewish. I explained why I wore such a necklace and witnessed to him of my love for Israel and the Jewish people. I told him I was a member of a group of Christians from my church who met monthly to learn more about their Jewish roots and to pray for Israel. I added that I was going to Israel in just two months with Christian Friends of Israel.

Even though I was feeling the pain, I lay there thinking, "God, is this why I am here?" I knew this encounter was no coincidence. The accident was my fault, but I knew God was in charge of this moment. The young man said his father was Jewish, that he believed in Jesus. Still, he had never heard a Christian speak as I did about God's covenant promises to Israel. When he asked where I went to church, I suddenly remembered that another member of my church, a physician who had been on the trip to Jamaica with me, was an emergency room doctor on staff at that very same hospital. What an extraordinary coincidence! What did all this mean? I am just an ordinary person. Why was I singled out for divine intervention that night? I believe that the angel in the car protected me because of God's purpose for my life. The Bible says in Romans 8:28 that "God causes all things to work together for good to those who love God, to those who are called according to His purpose."

If I had broken a bone, suffered a head trauma, or had any other major injury, I would not be able to go on the 2001 trip to Israel with Christian Friends of Israel. I would not have worked at the Joseph Storehouse, nor returned with CFI's Mission of Solidarity trip into the disputed territories later that same year. I would not have met the Gawel brothers whose ministry in Poland captured my heart; planted a seed, and laid the groundwork for my visit to Poland in 2007. In Poland, I got to know Janet Morgan. Her comment lit a fire in me to search out the Jewish connection to my Huguenot ancestors, which ultimately led to my writing this book.

Appendix

My DNA Result

In 2012, I sent a sample of my blood to National Geographic to be DNA-tested. What I found at that time was limited to DNA markers connecting me to the same DNA markers of Jewish descent.

From National Geographic:

Indigenous DNA (BETA) Search indigenous populations in scientific journals. The DNA markers of Judy Davis were compared to a dataset of 345 populations in 24 journals (location 16090 to 16340). The closest matches in a set of 345 populations are listed in the tables, the largest numbers first: I listed only a sample from an extremely long list of Jewish DNA markers linking my DNA to these people groups.

6 Ashkenazi Jews	RMI	35,355
Ashkenazi Jews (origin as Poland)	RMI	20,899
Ashkenazi Jews (origin as Lithuania)	RMI	17,471
Ashkenazi Jews (origin as Russia)	RMI	16,476
Sephardic Jews		1,071
Sephardic (Basques of Northern Spain)		1,261
Sephardic (Galicians of Spain)		1,083

The threads running throughout the people groups in my DNA leads me to believe that my ancestors were descended from the Southern tribe of Judah. I say this because the Crypto-Jews arriving in France and throughout Europe during the expulsion of Jews from Spain and other places were not descended from the ten northern tribes who had been so assimilated and absorbed that they had lost their identity—Meaning no longer practicing Jews, so that they could not be identified as such for purposes of persecution. So they were most likely Jews from the Southern kingdom of Judah and Benjamin, taken from Jerusalem by the Romans instead of the Assyrians who were absorbed into many different cultures and scattered throughout the world and lost their identity. (For instance, Paleo Indian tribes in America.

The Davis Connection

Davis (David, Davys, Davidson) is Jewish in origin, not Welsh, as traditional thought has it. In the online article, "Arise Huguenot Prophets and Light the Lamp," the author states that the Davises were brought to Wales by the Romans. Still, their origin lies elsewhere in the Middle East. It is now thought that the Davis roots go all the way back to Palestine—their ancestors were Jewish.

My great-grandmother, who married Richard Randolph Michaux, was Sallie Davis. Of course, my husband is a Davis on the paternal side and a German Huguenot on his mother's side.

The Michaux Data

Abraham Michaux, the progenitor of the Michaux family in Virginia, was a Huguenot, born in Sedan, France, in 1672. On account of religious persecution, he left France for Amsterdam, Holland.

The records of Amsterdam's French church show that they became a member of that church on January 28, 1691, then married Suzanne Rochet on July 1, 1692 and had his children baptized, as follows:

Anne, May 7, 1693
Jean, January 3, 1697
Issac, June 28, 1699
Jacques, August 15, 1700

Abraham Michaux's mother was probably a Severin, as his Book of Common Prayer bears on its fly-leaf the inscription, "Monsr, Severin, Minister, sends this book of Common Prayer to his nephew, Abraham Michaux. This book, published in London is 1706, was presented to the Episcopal Theological Seminary, Alexandria, Virginia, in 1857, by N.F. Cabell.

The old family Bible, published in 1657, is now in possession of Mrs. Thomas Garden of Prince Edward County, Virginia. It contains the names and marriage records of the family of Abraham Michaux. His will, dated May 13, 1717, and proved August 5, 1717, in Henrico Co., Virginia, mentions his wife Suzanne and his children. To these, he left an estate consisting of lands in Henrico and plantation and land at Manakin Town. They were:

Jacob m. Judith Woodson, daughter of John W. and Mary Miller
John
Abraham
John Paul
Anne
Jane Magdalen
Olive Jude
Elizabeth
Anne Madelin
Ester Mary

Suzanne La Roche Rochet

Suzanne Rochet (so spelled in Holland records) was the daughter of Moses Rochet, of Sedan, France. During the religious persecution by the Catholics, Moses Rochet sent his daughter to Holland to prevent the priest from placing them in Catholic schools. The parents were in good circumstances and were allowed to pay a yearly ransom to the French government to be permitted to live there in peace as Protestants, but this place did not include the children.

The story of the hazardous escape of Suzanne is told in Dr. W.F. Foote's *The French Huguenot*. The parents often visited their children in Holland taking with them money with which to buy silks and fine clothing, and it grieved them very much to see their daughters eating the coarse food of Holland.

Suzanne Rochet Michaux died in 1744, and her will is recorded in Goochland Co., Virginia.

From the Richmond Times-Dispatch, October 23, 1904:

Joseph Michaux, son of Jacob, was born Oct. 30, 1739, died Feb. 8, 1807; married Judith Woodson, b. March 23, 1747, d. Aug. 16, 1803. On Oct. 9, 1761, served as Captain in the Revolutionary War for American Independence. His wife, Judith Woodson, was the daughter of John Woodson and his wife Mary Miller, of Lancaster County, Va, who were married Aug. 10, 1731. Joseph Michaux's children were:

Jacob, b. Jan. 12, 1764 ---died in 1828
Betsy, b. July 11, 1766 ---d. Feb. 1784
John, b. Dec,23, 1768 ---d. Oct. 19, 1817
Joseph, b. Apr. 3, 1771 ---d. Sept. 1837
Jesse, b. Apr. 27, 1773
Daniel W., b. Aug. 24, 1775
Richard W., b. Feb. 18, . 14, 1779
Henrietta Rochet, b. Feb. 15, 1782
Obadiah W., b. Aug. 14, 1785
Judith W., b. Dec. 13, 1788

Joseph Michaux, b. Apr. 3, 1771, s. Awpr. 1837, m. Feb.2, 1808 (first) Mrs. Judith A. Mosby. b. May 31, 1785, d. July 11, 1817. Their children were:
Judith Elizabeth, b. Dec. 11, 1808
Jane Caroline Lavinia, b. Nov. 6, 1810
Lucy Ann Harriet Rochet, b. Apr. 3, 1812
Martha Joseph Henry, b. July 20, 1814
Joseph George, b. Oct. 8, 1815

Appendix

Second marriage of Joseph Michaux, Feb. 7, 1822, m. Anne Meade Randolph, daughter of Brett Randolph, Jr. of Powhatan Co., VA. Their children were:

Richard Randolph, b. Jan. 22, 1823 Cumberland County VA. d. Nov. 20, 1899 at Liberty, NC.
   John LaFayette, b. Sept. 3, 1824 ---d. July 6, 1898
   Daniel Meade, b. Sept 1, 1826 --- d. in 1899

Richard Randolph Michaux m. Anna Davis of Hargrove Co., NC. Their children were:
Anna Meade, b. c.
John Randolph, b. c. ---d. San Francisco, b. 1909

His second marriage to Sarah Anderson Davis (sister to Anna) of Hargrove Co., NC. Their children were:
William Wilson, b. 1883
Martha Rochet, b. 1885
Brett Davis, b. 1886
Mable Clare, b. 1888
Lucile Duty, b. 1890
Sarah Garnett, b. 1895

Mabel Clare Michaux (my grandmother) married Luther Waugh McKinney. They moved from Liberty, NC to Westfield on Sauratown Mtn. in Stokes Co., NC. Their children were:
Lillian Lucille
Brett Dilworth
Frances Michaux
Mary Meade
Laura Ruth

Date records for the birth, death, and marriage of Lillian Lucille, Brett Dilworth, and Laura Ruth could not be found.

Lillian Lucille McKinney first married Enoch Vanderpool, and their marriage was later dissolved. They had two children:
Charles Enoch
Richard Michaux

Lillian Lucille's second marriage was to Donald Honeycutt, and they had no children.

Brett Dilworth McKinney's first marriage to Gloria (last name unknown) was later dissolved. They had no children.

Brett Dilworth's second marriage was to Letha Cooper, and they had one child:
Zandra Lynn

Laura Ruth McKinney married William (Bill) Gillespie. They had three children:
Charles Brett
Sandra (middle name unknown)
Billie Sharon

Frances Michaux McKinney (b. 1923- d. 2001) married William Vester (Dock) Marshall, (b. 1917- d. 1995.) They had two children:
Brenda Caron, b. Nov. 21. 1942
Judy Gail, b. Dec. 2, 1944

Brenda Caron Marshall married Douglas Ray Mckinney, Oct. 27, 1961. They had two sons:
Zane Ray, b. Sept. 8, 1968
Chadwick Dale, b. March 16, 1970

Judy Gail Marshall married Jesse Shumate Davis, Jr. June 11, 1967. They had two sons:
Jesse Shumate, III
John Marshall

Mary Meade McKinney married Russell Stevens. They had one child:
Charlotte Ann, b. August 8, 1947

Charlotte Ann Stevens first married Steve Martin, June 6, 1965. The marriage was later dissolved. They had one daughter:
Ann Michelle, b. March 10, 1967

Charlotte Ann Stevens second marriage was to Mike Lawson June 20, 1976. They had one son:
Daniel Christopher, b. Dec. 4, 1979

My great aunt Lucille Duty Michaux m. Norton Wardlaw Brooker of Columbia, SC on Dec. 15, 1920, in Asheville, NC at the home of her half-sister, Anna Meade and her husband, the Rev. James Samuel Williams. Their child was:
Nancy Michaux, b. Oct 11, 1921

Nancy Michaux Brooker m. Alvin W. Bronwell of DeKalb, IL on June 21, 1943. The marriage was dissolved in March 1975.

The Michaux-Pocahontas Connection

My Native American bloodline co-mingled with Huguenot blood back with the entrance of Joseph Michaux into the family line through his marriage to Anne Meade Randolph. I will now present the lineage through Anne Meade Randolph (daughter of cousins Ann and Brett Randolph, Jr.) back to Edward the III, King of England, who reigned from 1327 to 1377, the year of his death.

Examining the Data Gained from the Huguenot Society

Moving backward from Nancy (Ann) Meade, who married Richard Randolph, Jr., we find their parents, Lady Susanna Everard and David Mead of Virginia. Lady Everard's parents were Sir Richard Everard, Bart, and Susanna Kidder (daughter of Richard Kidder, Bishop of Bath and Wells). Sir Richard Everard's parents were Sir

Hugh Everard, Bart, and Mary Brown. Sir Hugh Everard, Bart's parents, were Lady Joan Barrington and Sir Richard Everard Bart (1625). Lady Joan Barrington's parents were Sir Francis Barrington and Lady Joan Cromartie, daughter of Sir Henry Cromartie. Sir Francis Barrington's parents were Lady Winifred Pole and Thomas Barrington, High Sheriff of Essex.

Lady Winifred Pole's parents were Sir Henry Pole and Lady Jean Neville. Sir Henry Pole's parents were Lady Margaret Plantagenet and Sir Richard Pole, Knight of the Garter. Lady Margaret Plantagenet's parents were Richard Plantagenet and Lady Cicely de Neville, daughter of Ralph de Neville, Earl of Westmoreland. Richard Plantagenet's parents were Richard Plantagenet (Sr.) and Lady Anna Mortimer, daughter of Edward Mortimer, Earl of March, and Phillipa, daughter of Lionel, Duke of Clarence, son of Edward II. Richard Plantagenet's (Sr.) parents were Edward Plantagenet and Lady Isabel, daughter of Peter, King of Castile, Spain, Earl of Cambridge, and Duke of York. Edward Plantagenet's parents were Edward III and Lady Phillipa, daughter of William, Count of Hainault, and Joan of Valois, daughter of Phillip III of France. Under the influence of his brilliant mother, Edward III thrived and became one of the most powerful military kings in England. However, the strength of the Plantagenets died with him, and that lineage was forced to bow to the emerging strength of the Tudors in the virgin queen, Elizabeth, the daughter of King Henry VIII and Anne Boleyn.

Elizabeth never married and remained the last Tudor monarch. Without an heir, the crown looked to the lineage of her half-sister, Mary (daughter of King Henry the VIII and Katherine of Aragon). Queen Elizabeth had her cousin, Mary (Queen of Scotts), beheaded for treason in 1587, after 19 years of captivity in a variety of castles and houses in England.

Mary was Margaret Tudor's granddaughter. Henry VIII was Margaret Tudor's brother. Thus, Elizabeth's succession fell to the Scots and the only suitable heir, Mary's son, King James.

ABOUT THE AUTHOR

Judy Davis is a native North Carolinian. She has a passion for art, dance, and writing. She loves to paint in oil, watercolor, and acrylic, winning awards in all three mediums. Several of her pieces are privately owned by collectors in the triad area of Winston-Salem-High Point, and Hatteras Island as well as in Canada.

Her love of self-expression and creativity drew Judy into dressmaking, doll making, art in worship, dance choreography, and poetry. Her poems evoke emotions while are at the same time, informative and edgy. "Thy Word There Still," "The Church Primeval," and "The Return, A White Horse is Coming" are prime examples. She believes poetry is fun and cathartic and provides a place for a field of thought not easily expressed in any other way. Many years before developing a passion to dye silks, choreograph dance, and outfit a dance team, she took formal tap dancing lessons. From 8 until 10 years of age, she danced on stage in local schools, talent competitions, once on the radio, and twice on television.

In the late '80s, when associated artists of Winston-Salem began a program to take local artists into Forsyth County's Public School System to demonstrate and teach art to the children, Judy became the liaison between schools and individual artists.

In 1999, after doing volunteer work as a dental hygienist in Jamaica, she began traveling to various countries as a short-term missionary.

In 2001, she worked at The Joseph Storehouse/Vision for Israel in Abu Gosh, then traveled into the disputed territories with Christian Friends of Israel's Mission of Solidarity, visiting communities in Ariel, Shiloh, Hebron, and the Golan Heights.

Judy lives near Winston-Salem, North Carolina. She has two sons, a daughter-in-law, and two granddaughters.

www.ingramcontent.com/pod-product-compliance
Lightning Source LLC
Chambersburg PA
CBHW070544010526
44118CB00012B/1220